Unicorns Adult Coloring Book Vol 3

60 Entertaining Stress Relieving Unicorn Patterns

By Omar Johnson

I0499739

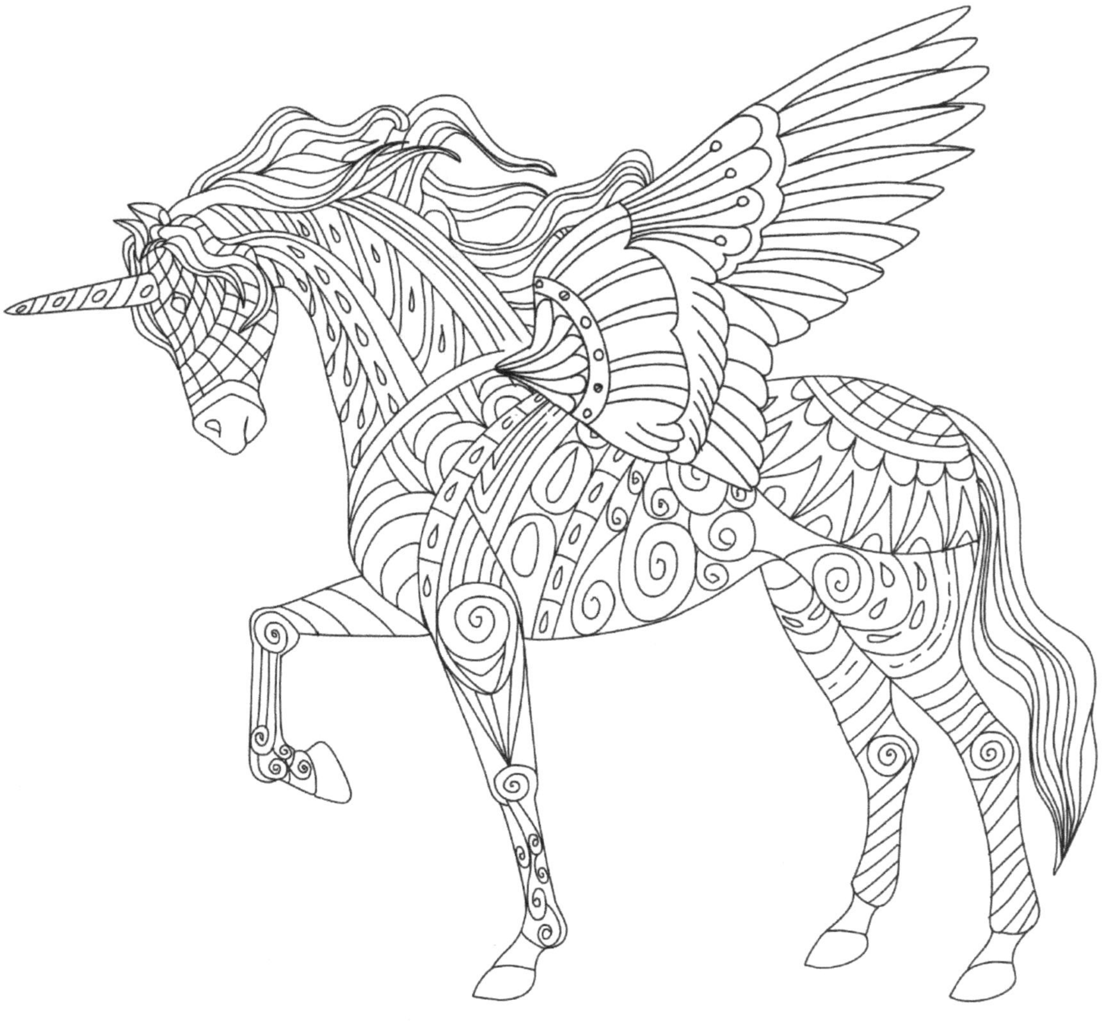

Get Your Free Butterfly Mandala Coloring Book

Visit

HTTPS://WWW.ADULTCOLORINGBOOKSFORYOU.COM

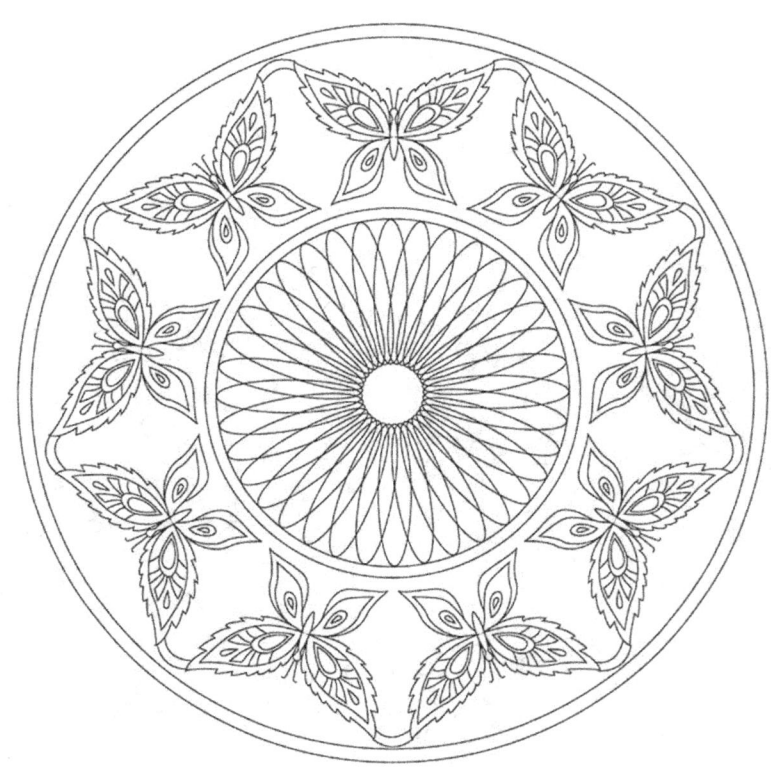

Make Profits Easy LLC Publishing

omarjohnson@adultcoloringbooksforyou.com

Copyright 2019

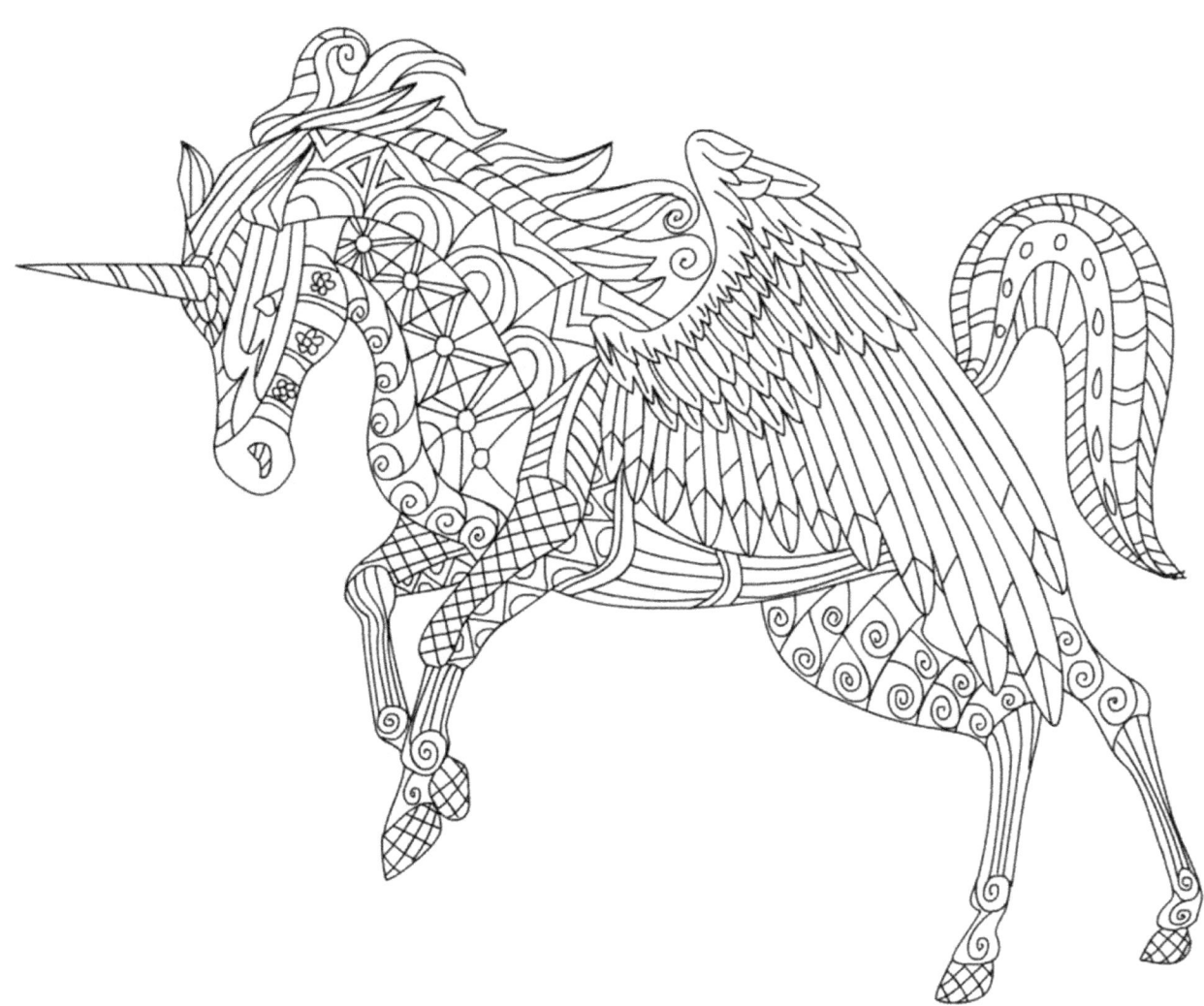

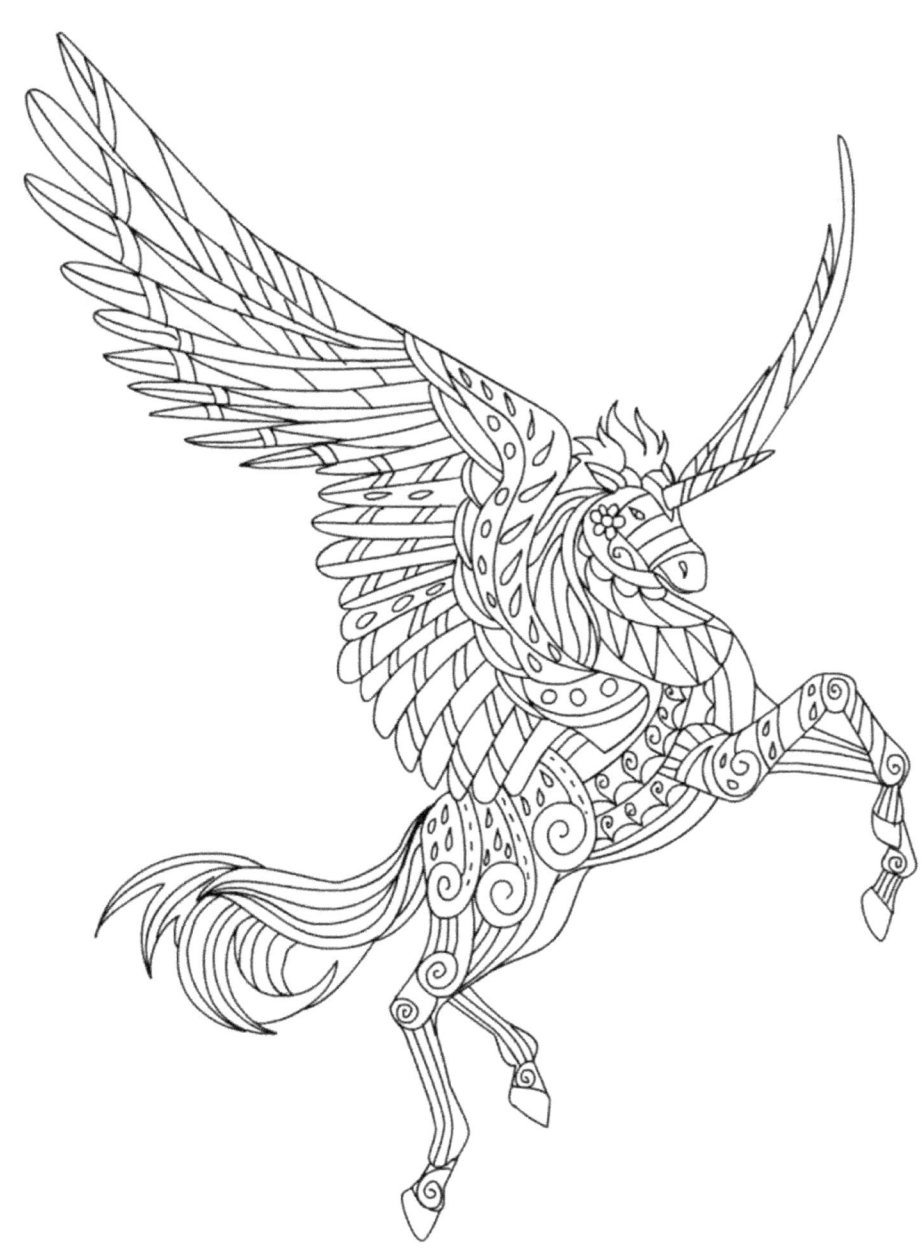

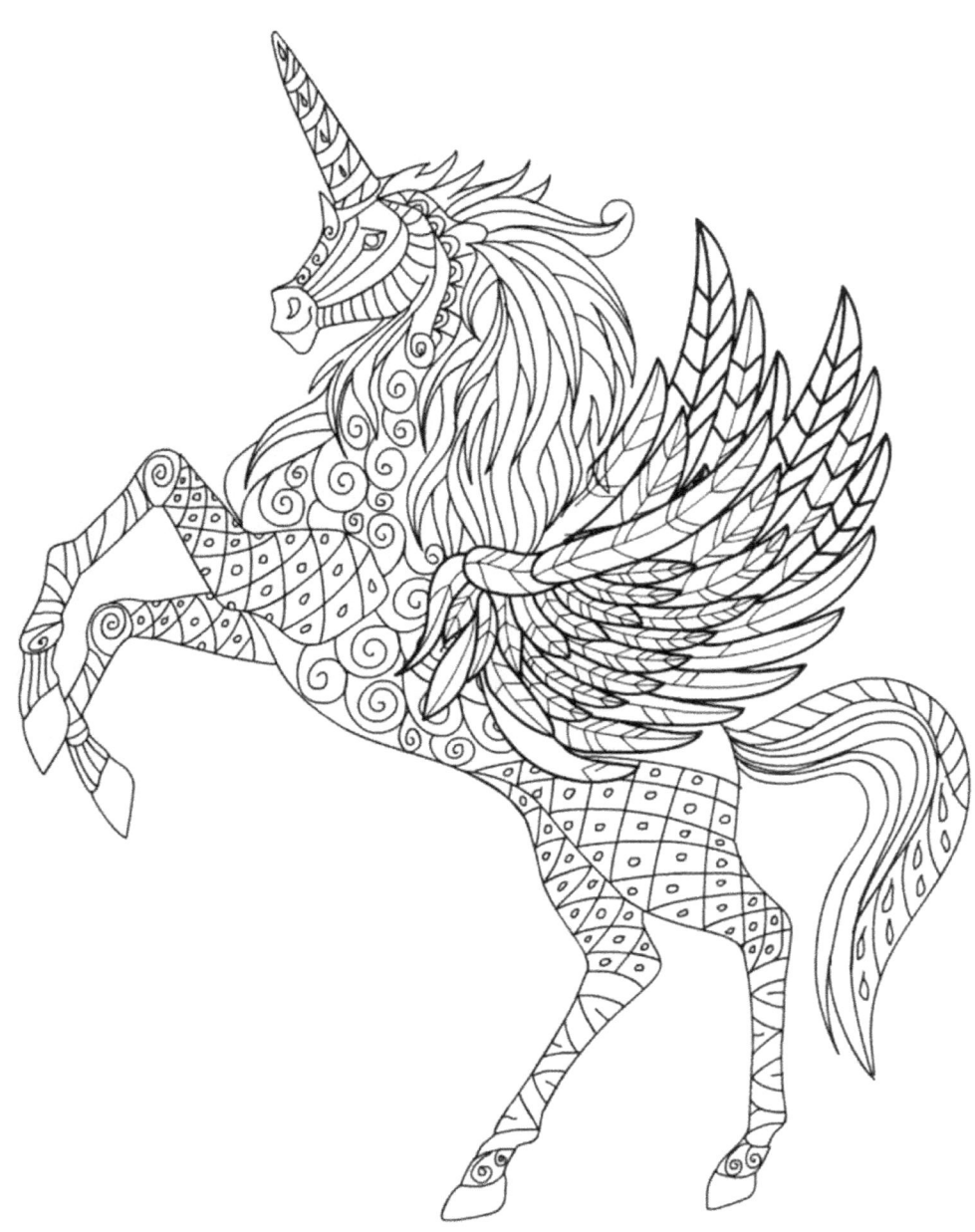

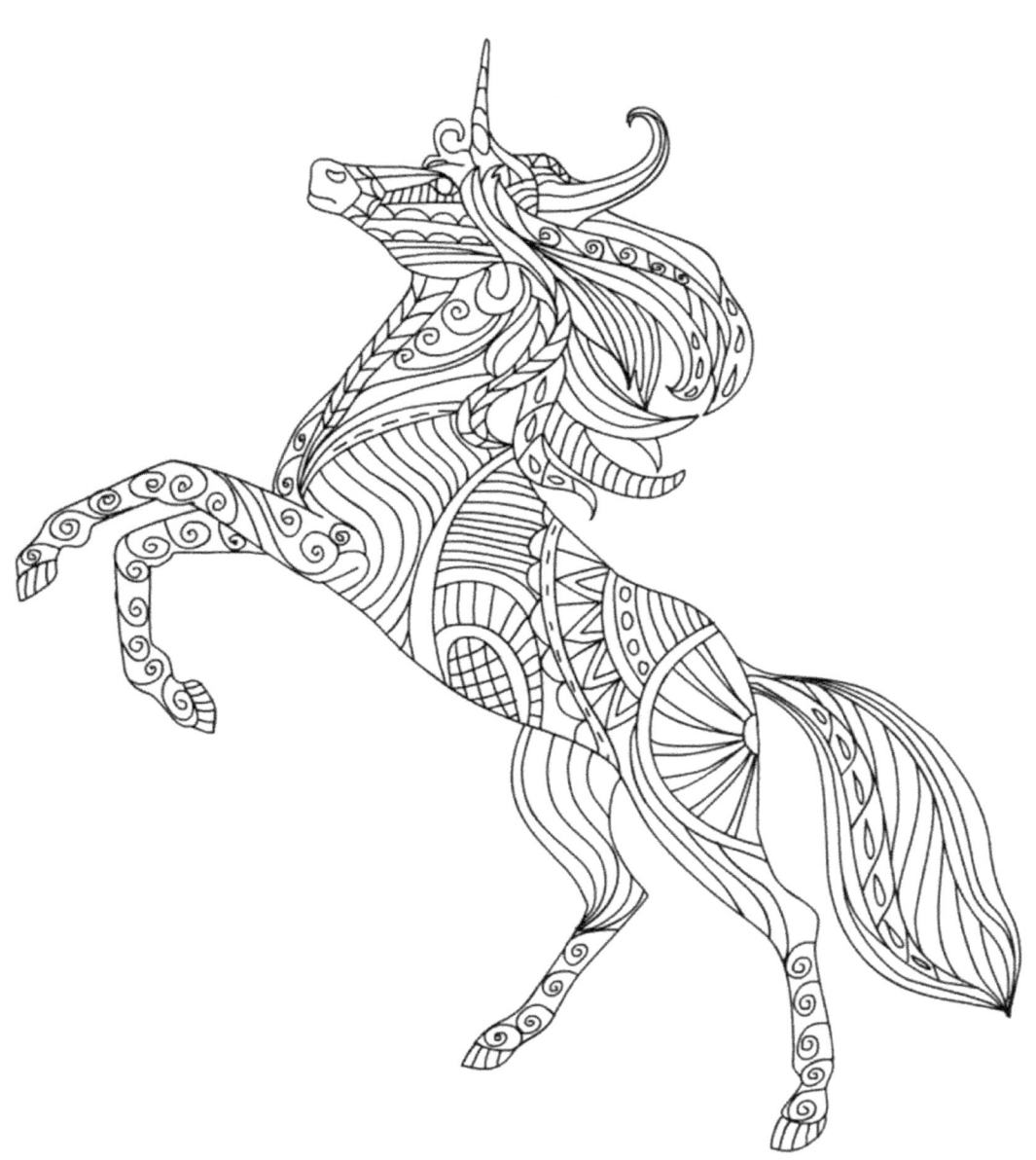

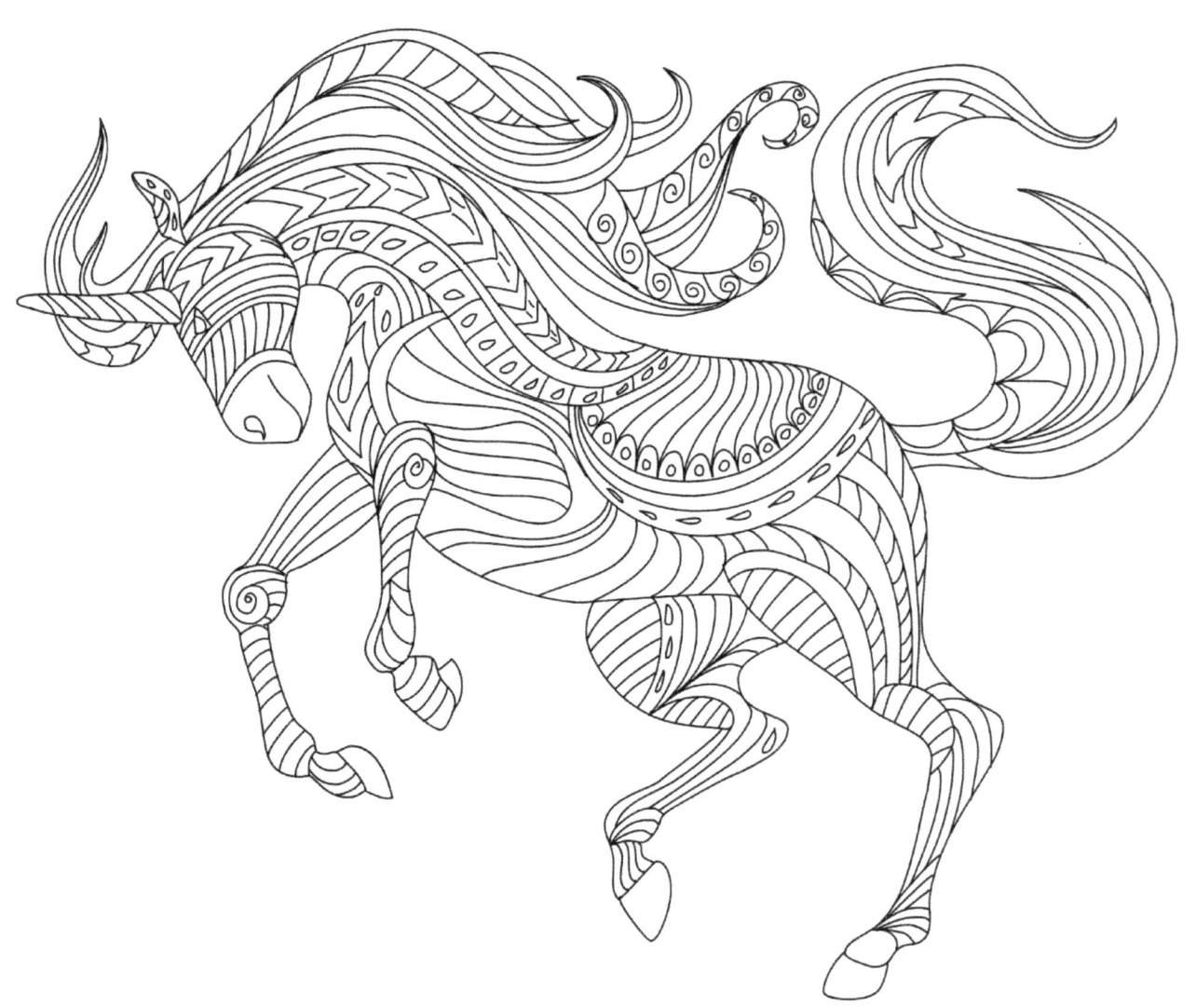

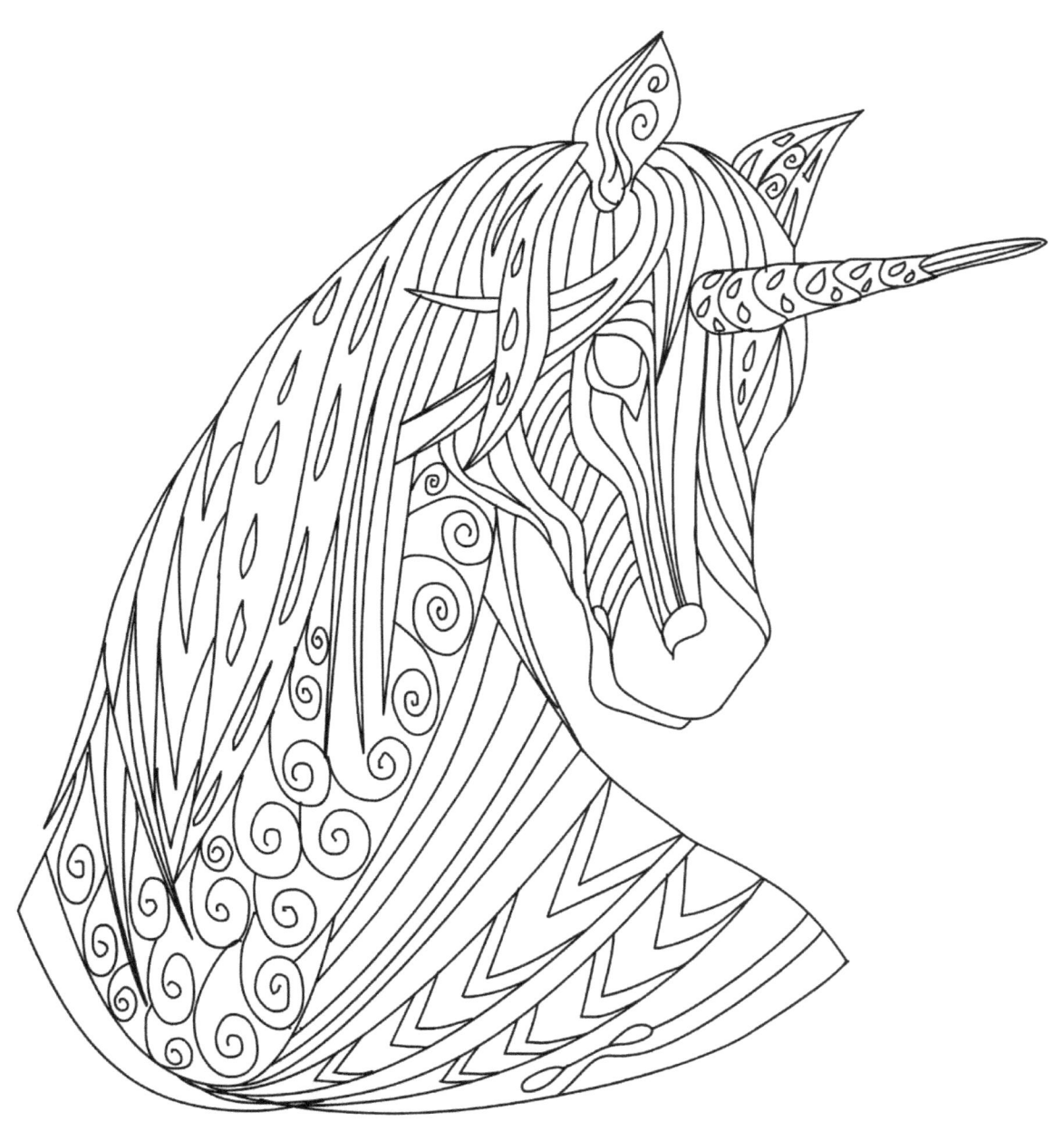

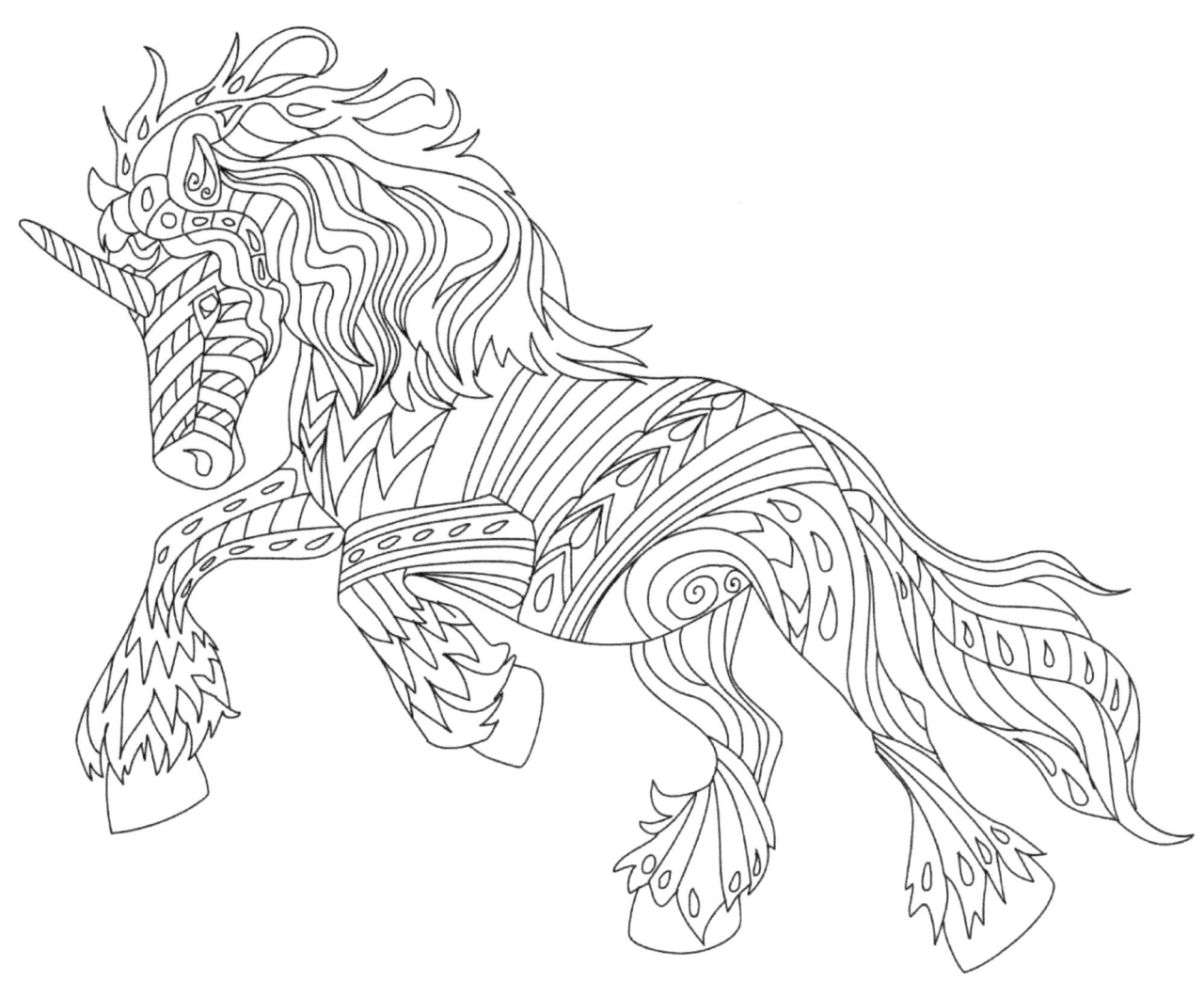

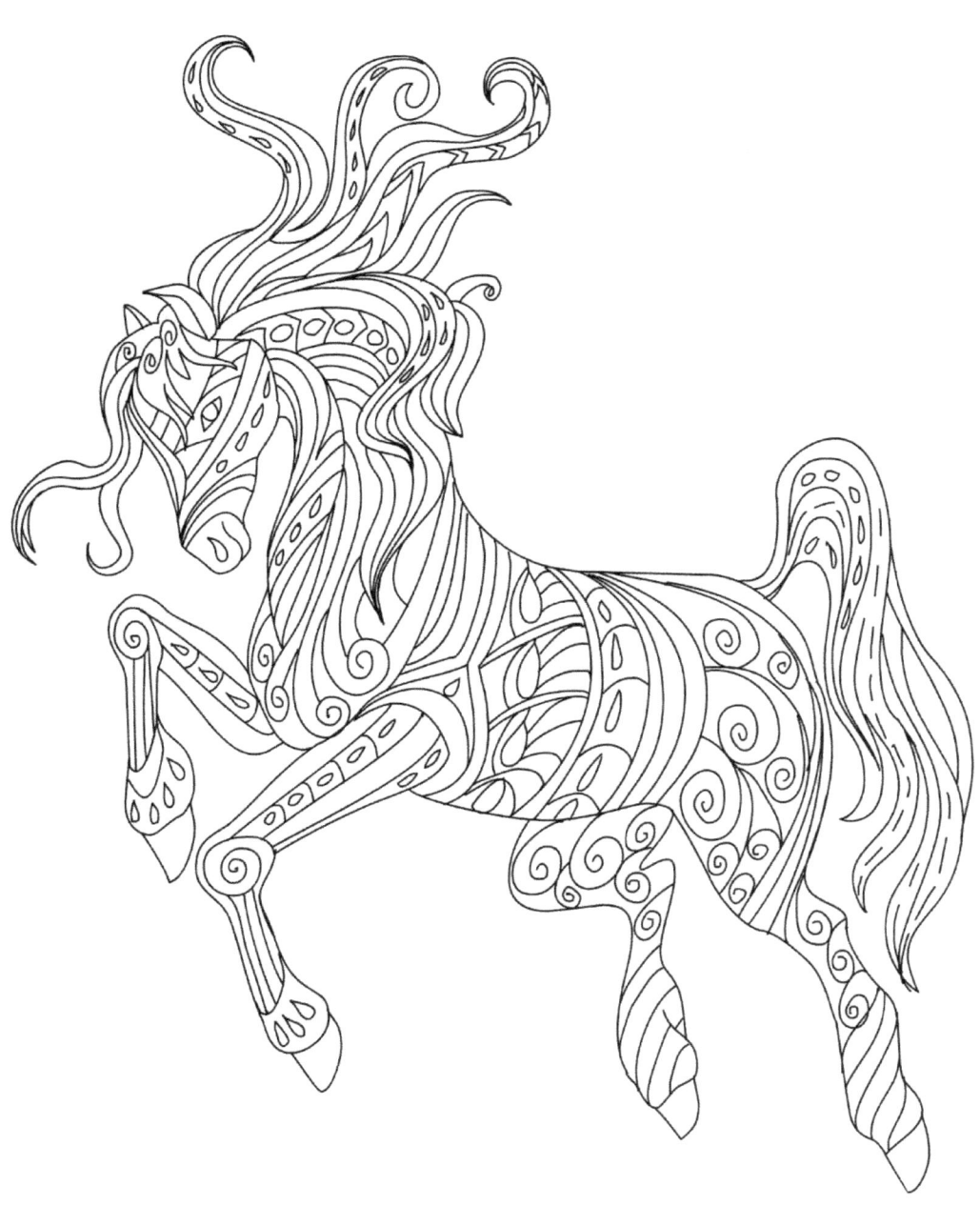

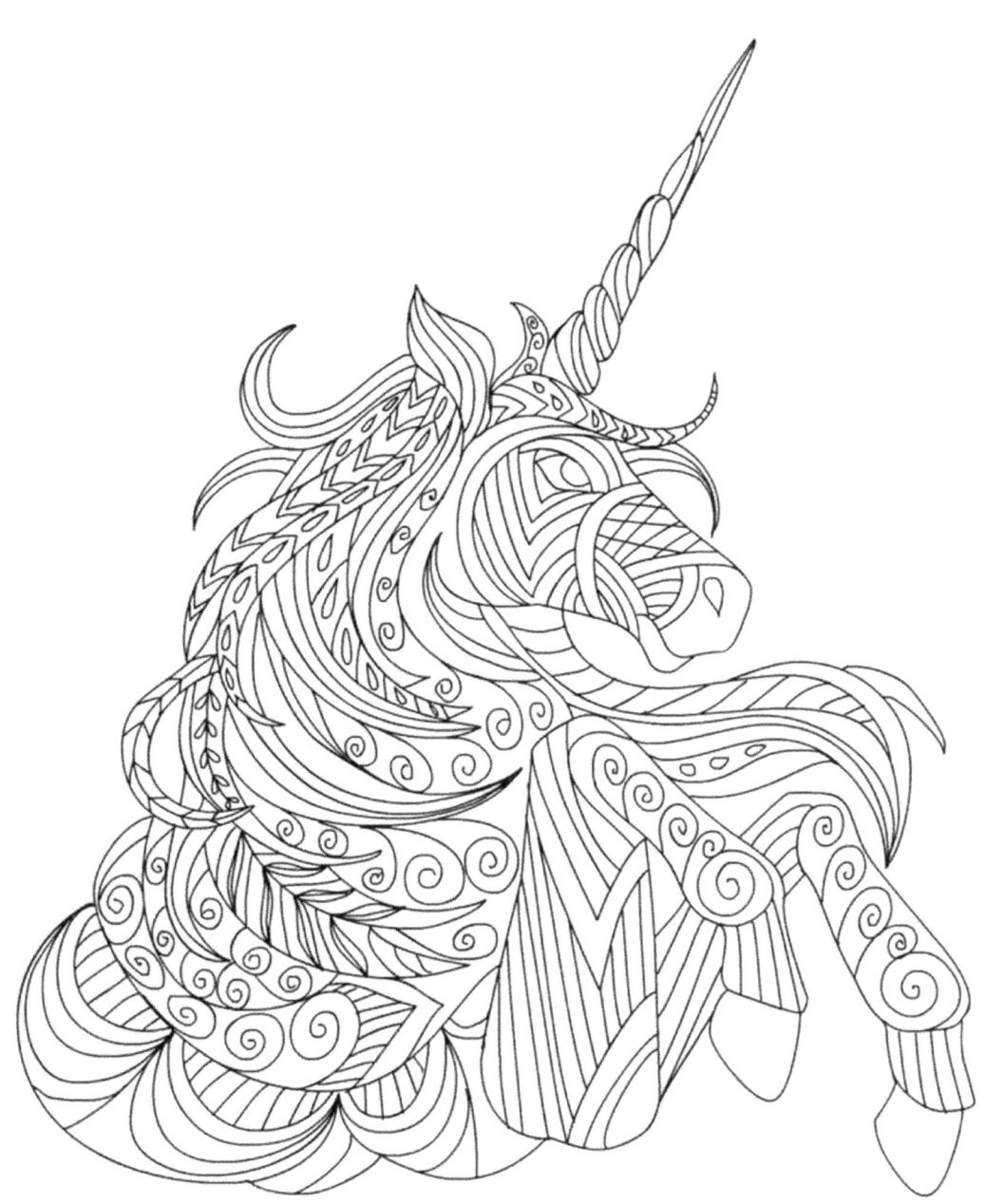

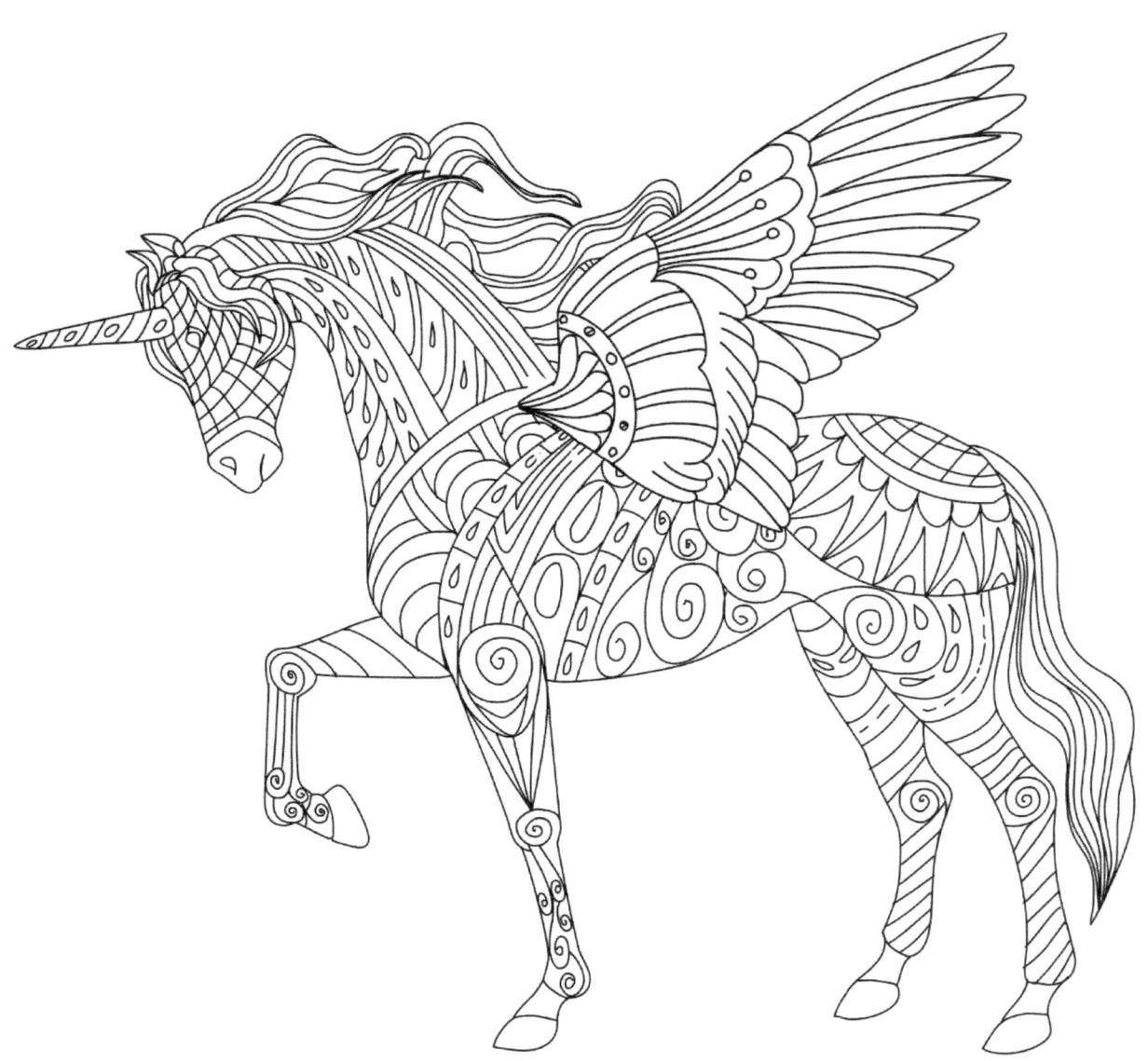

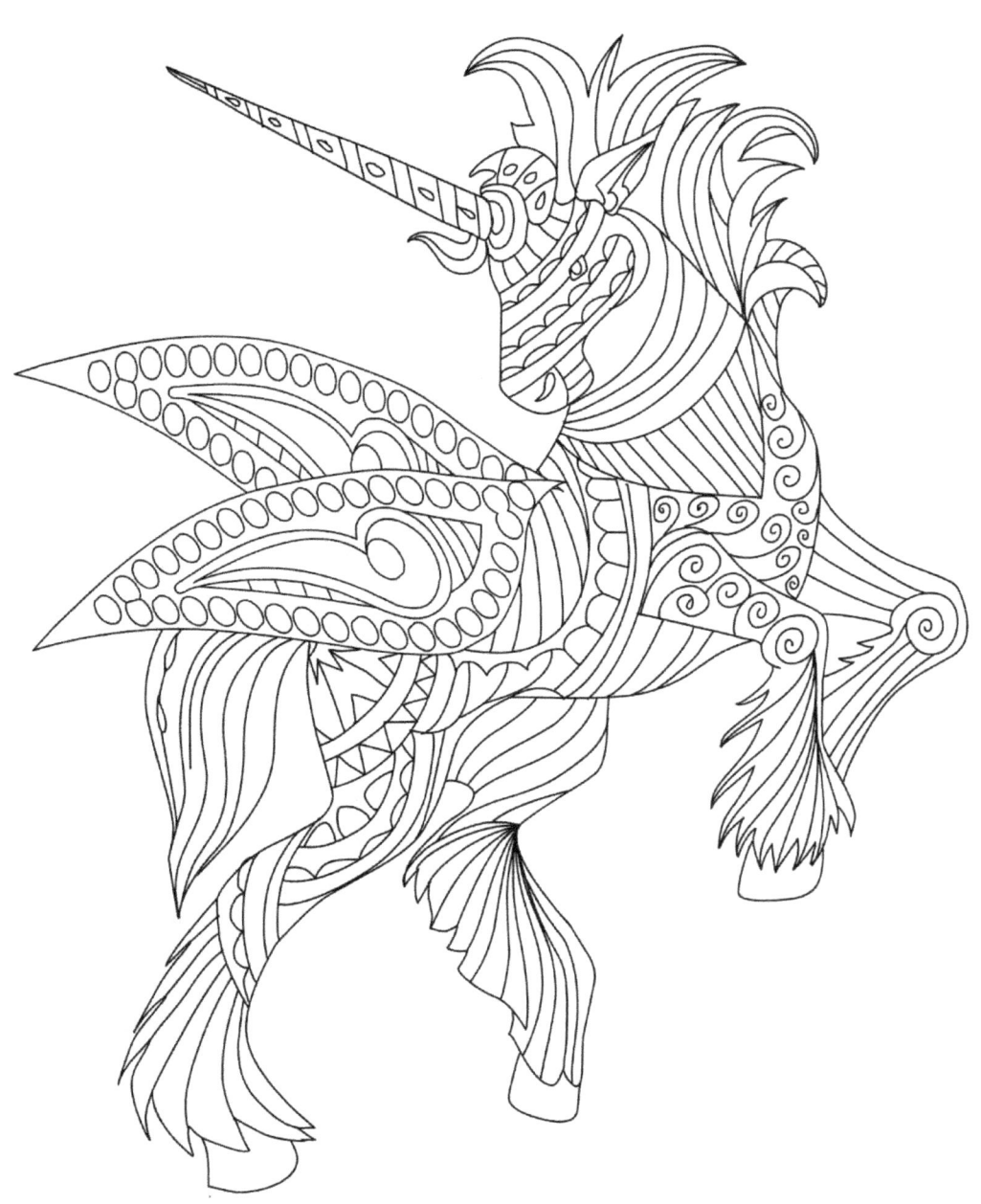

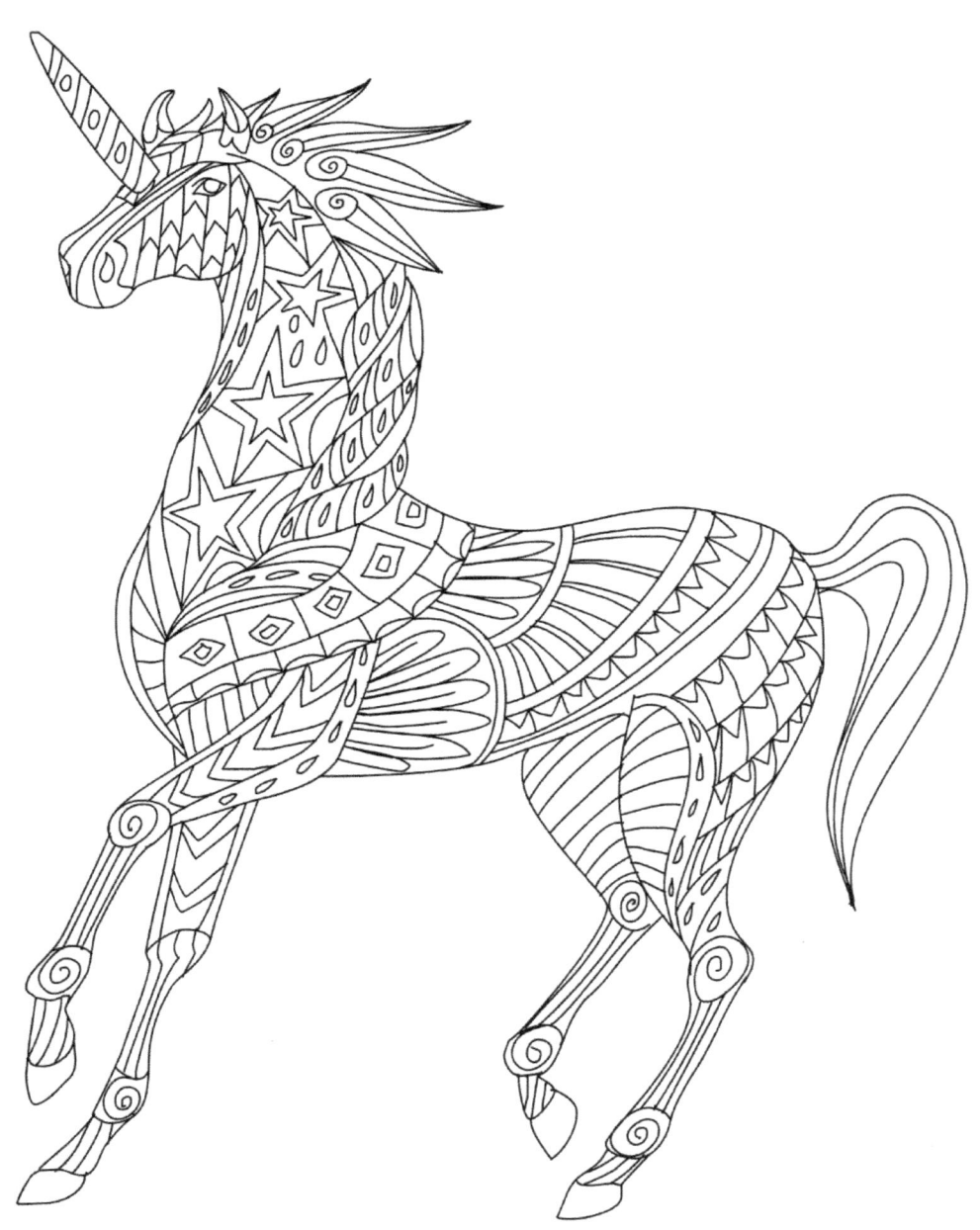

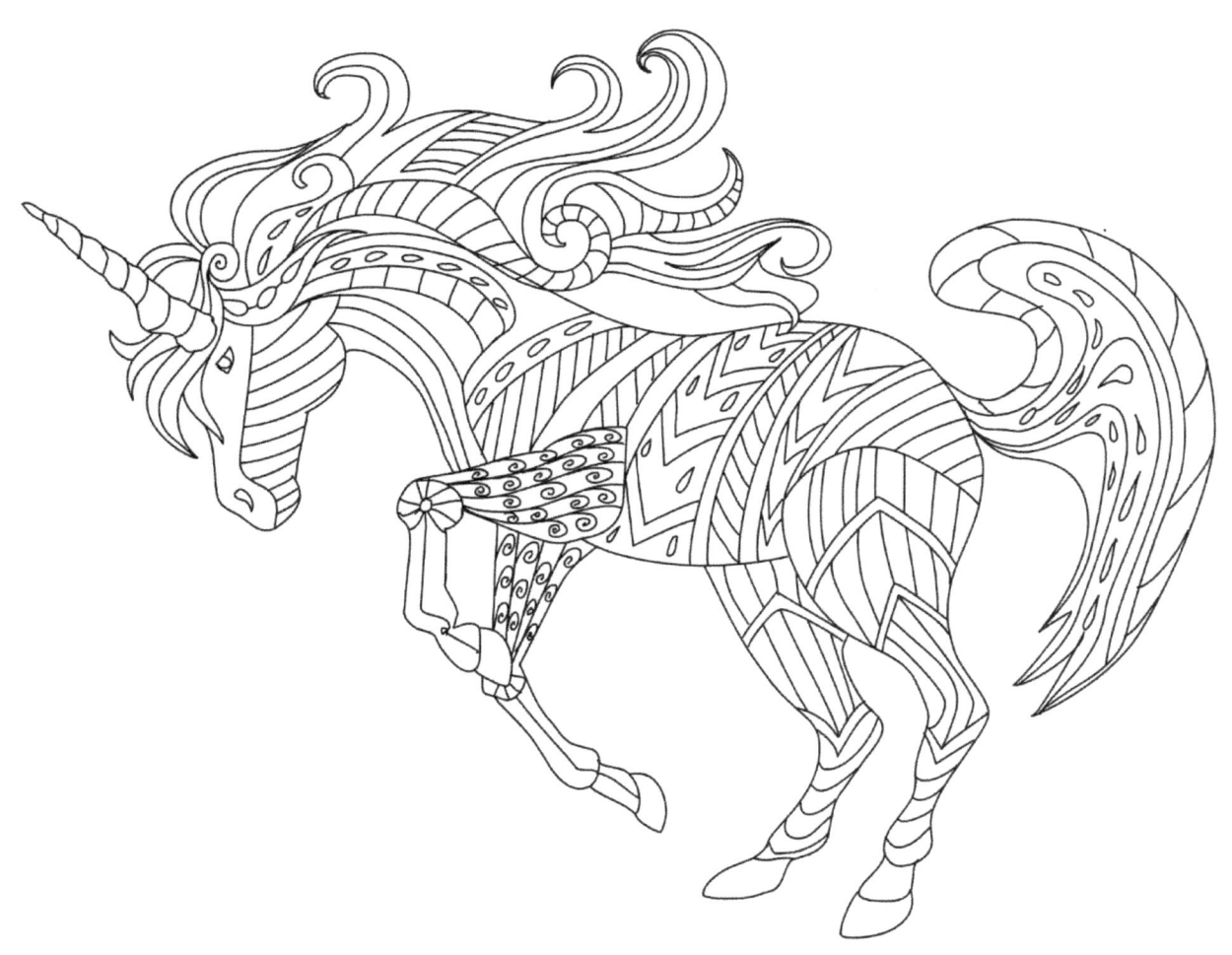

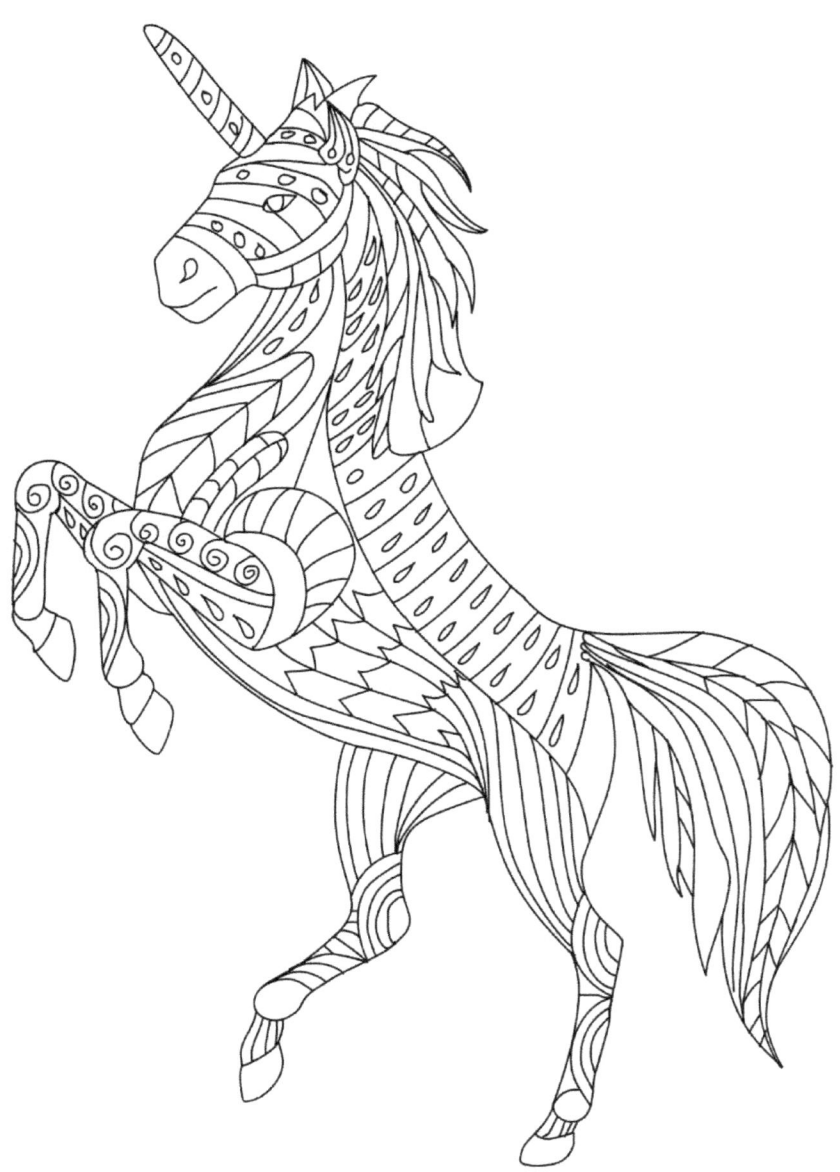

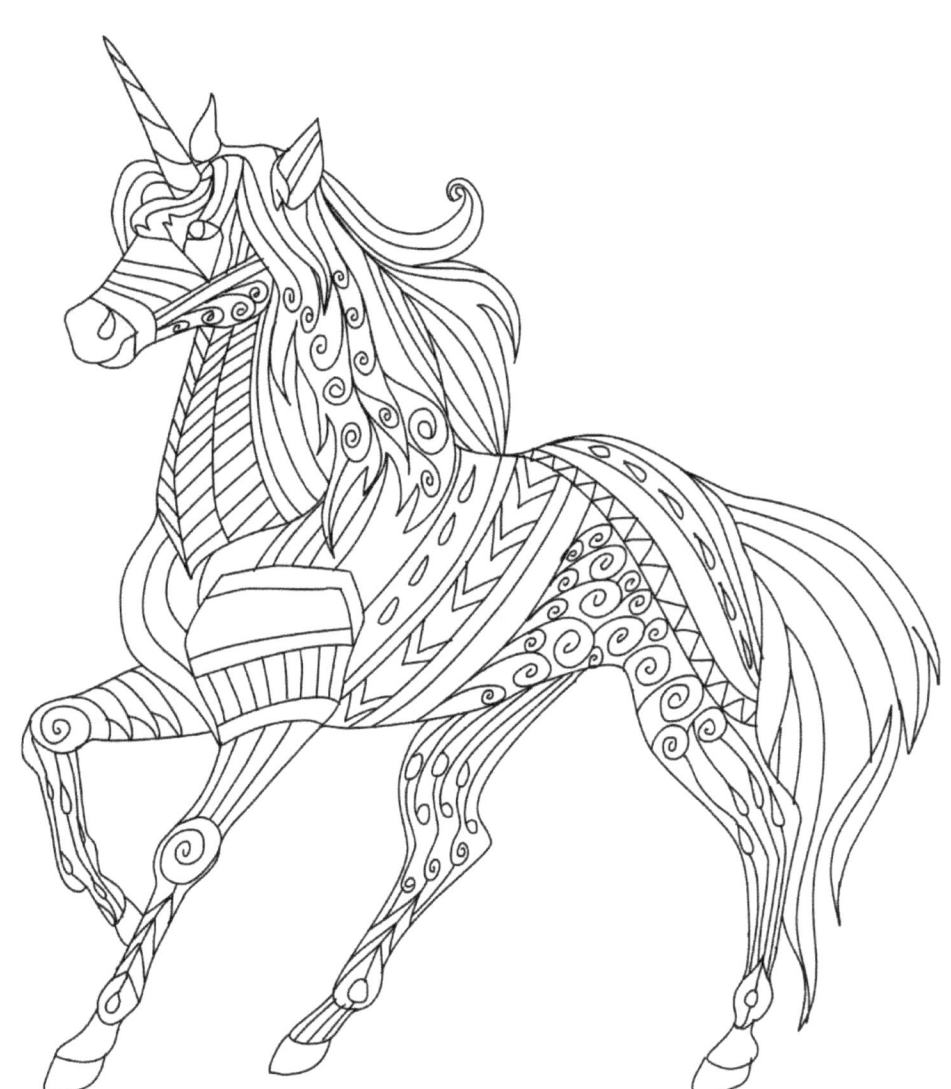

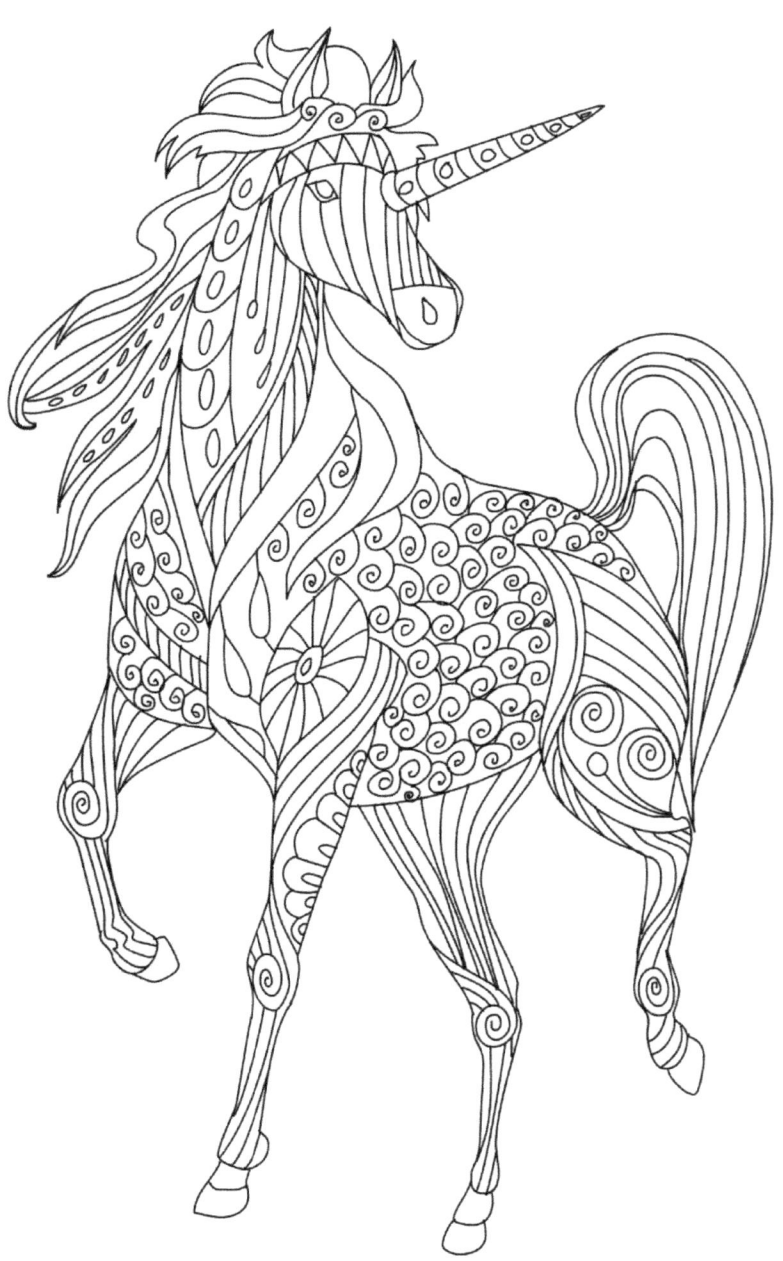

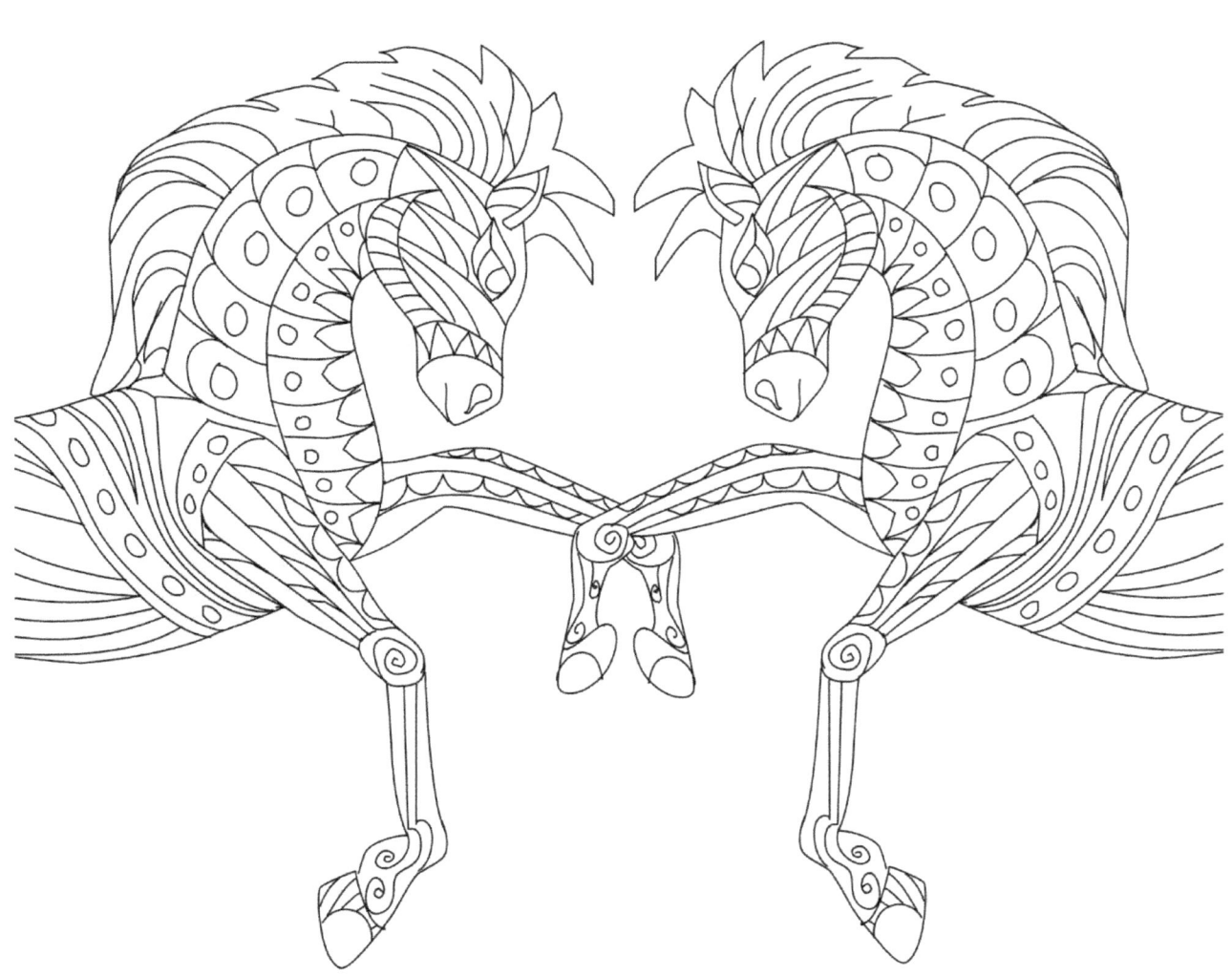

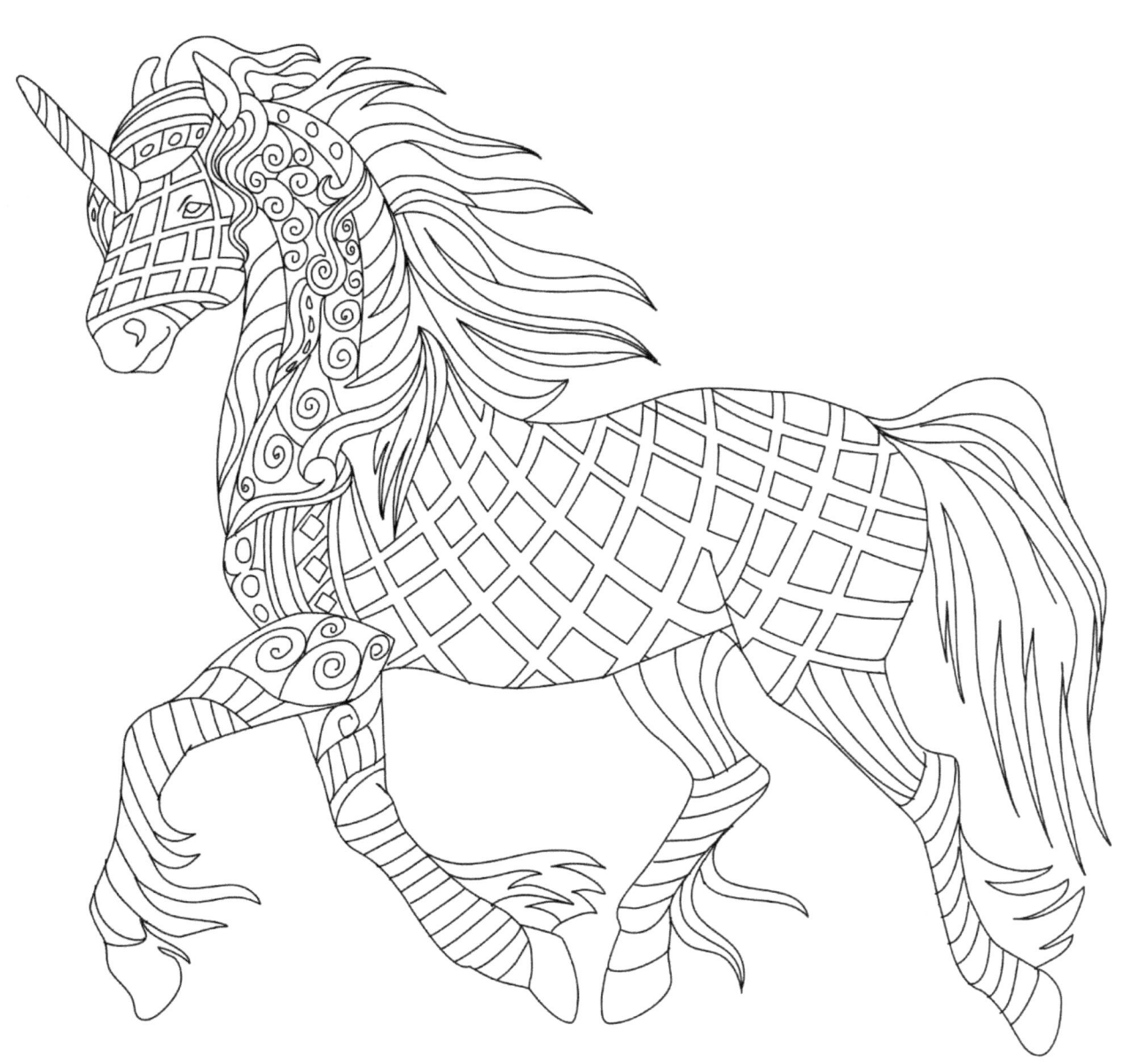

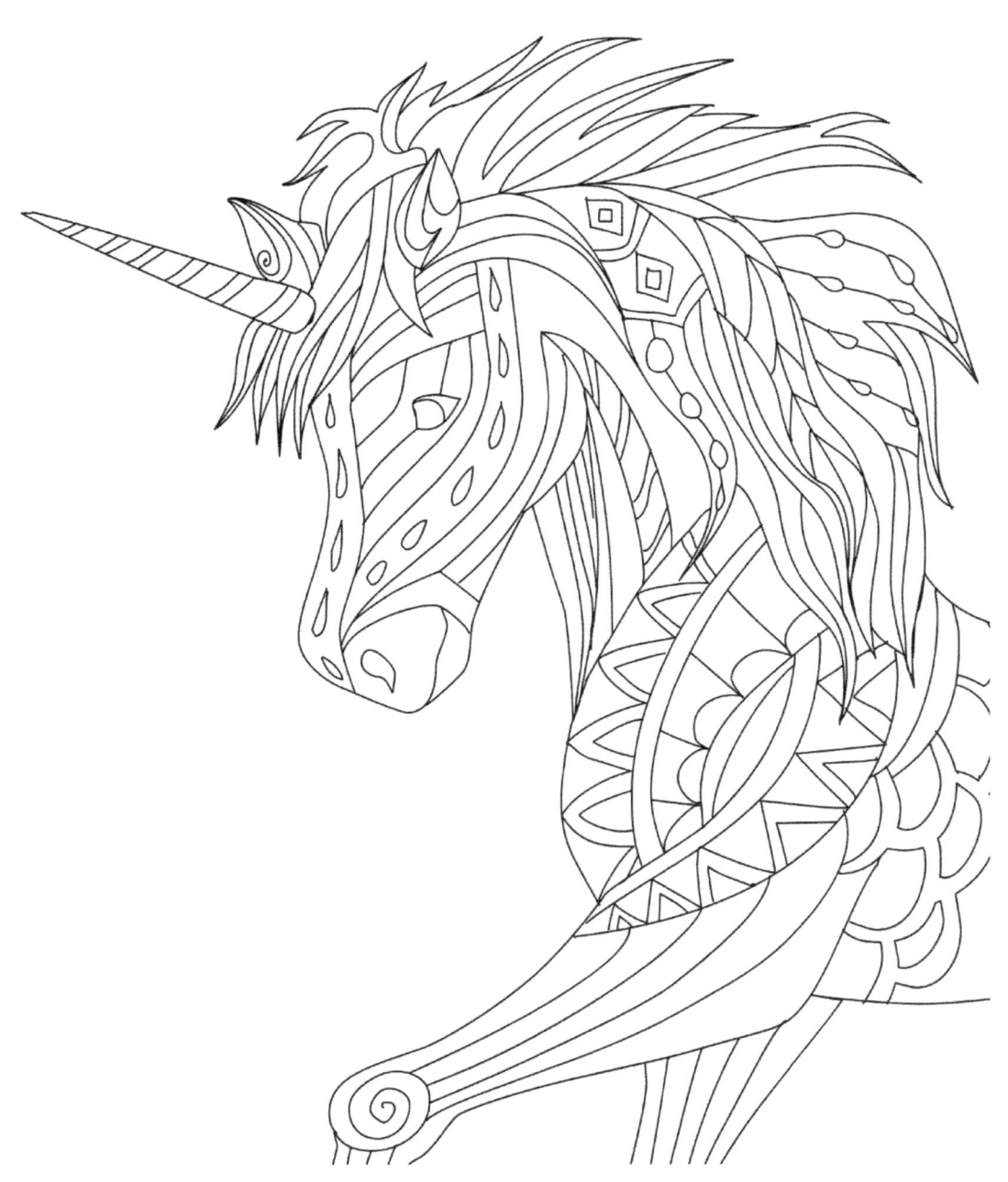

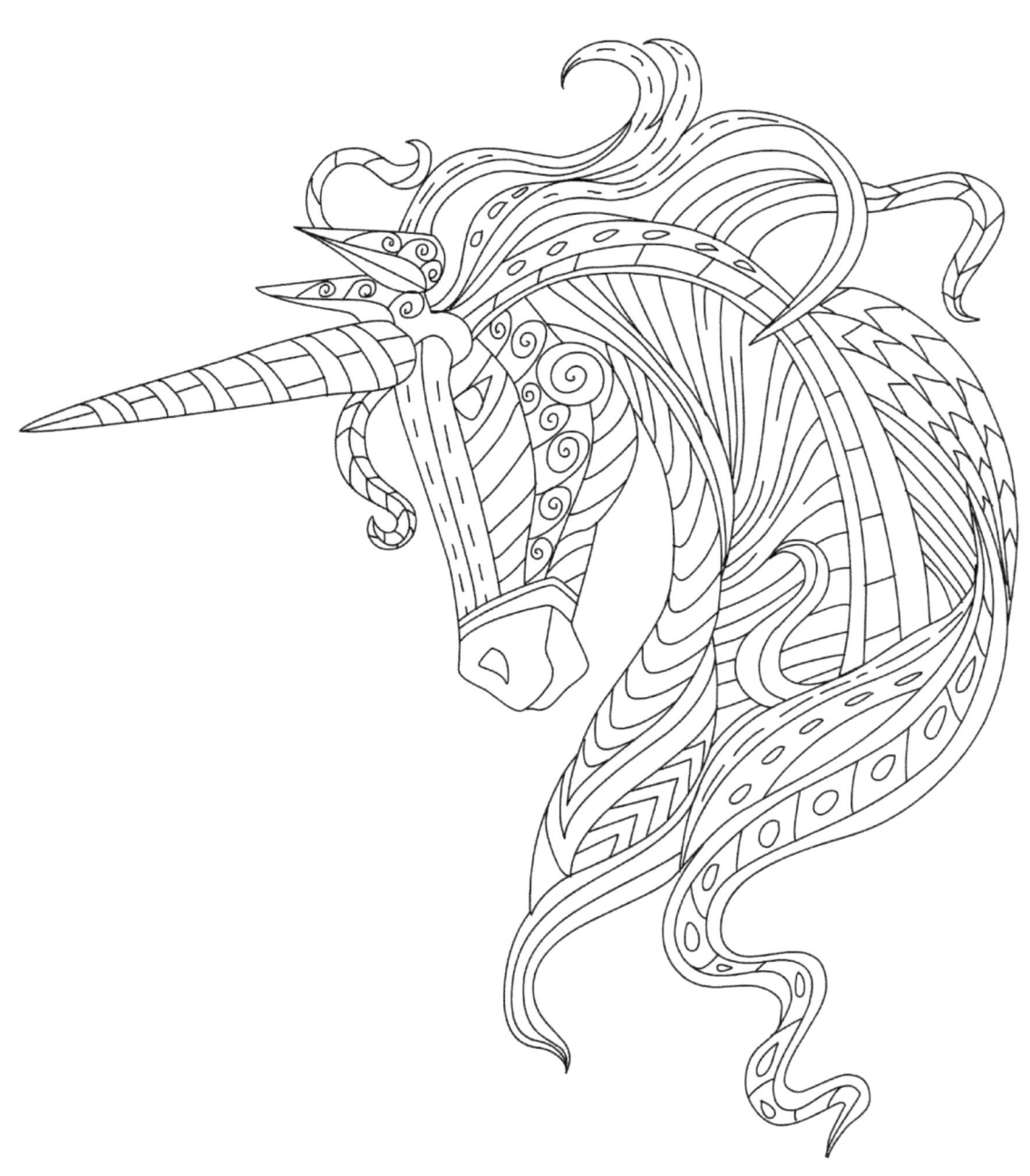

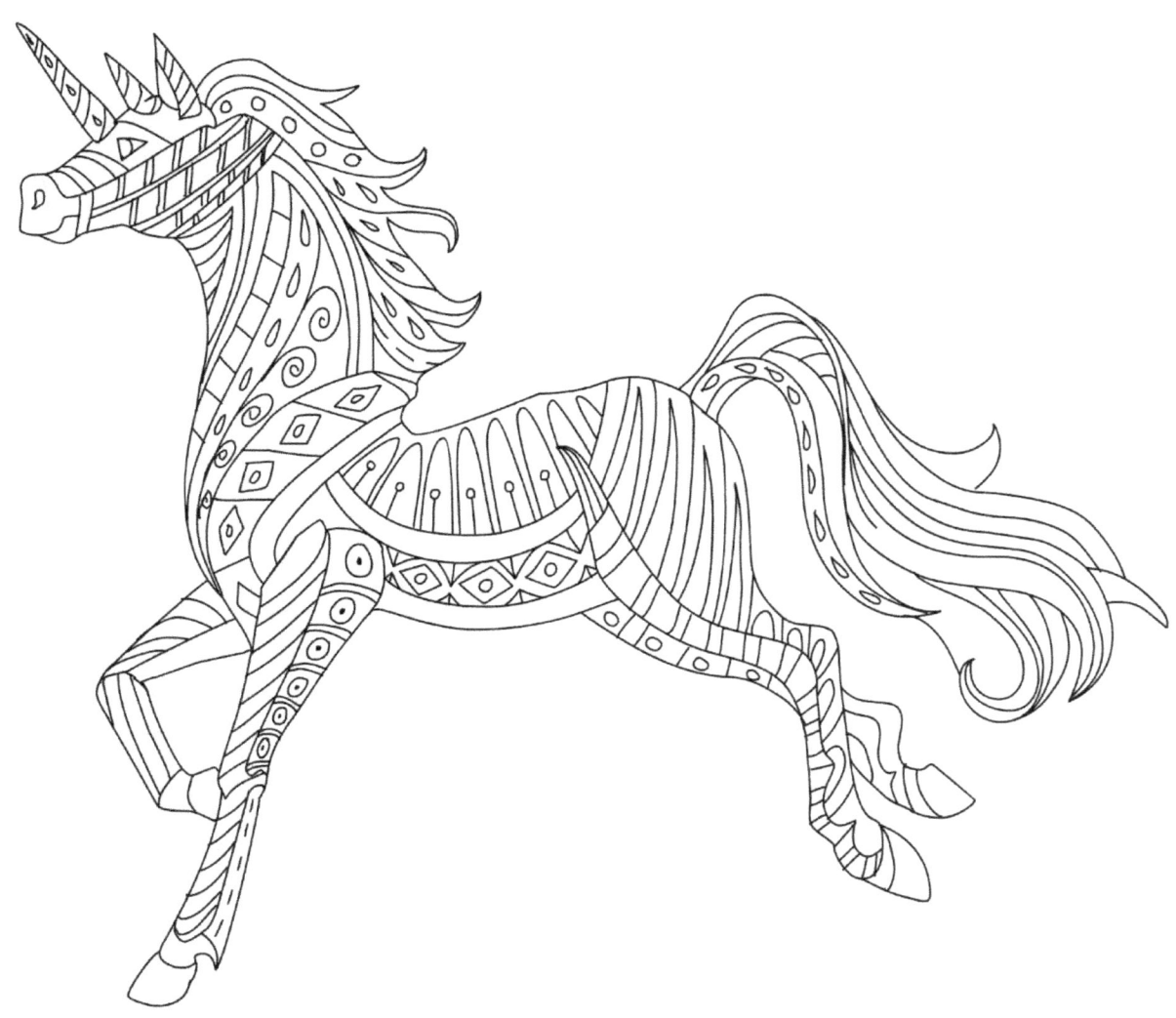

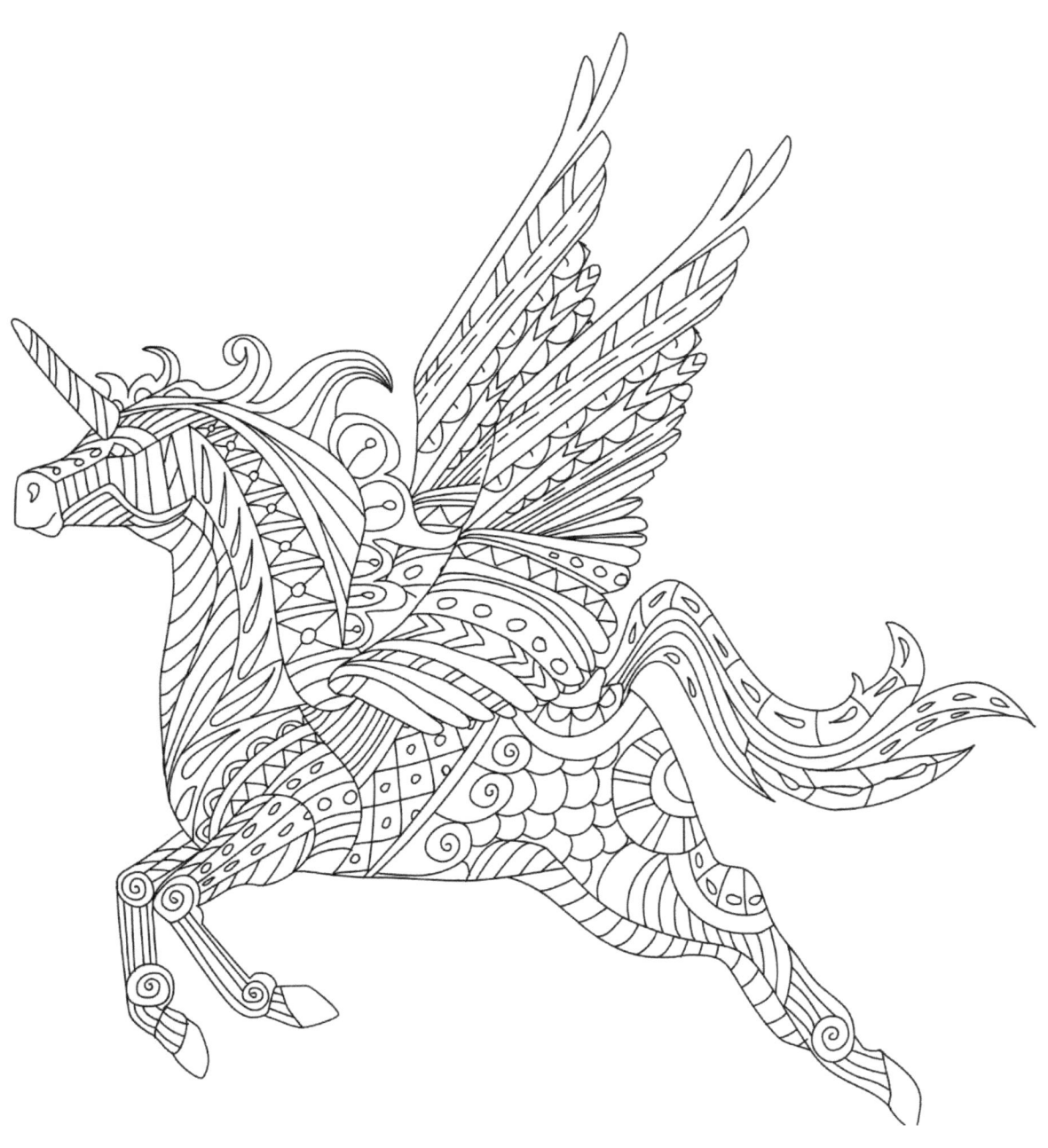

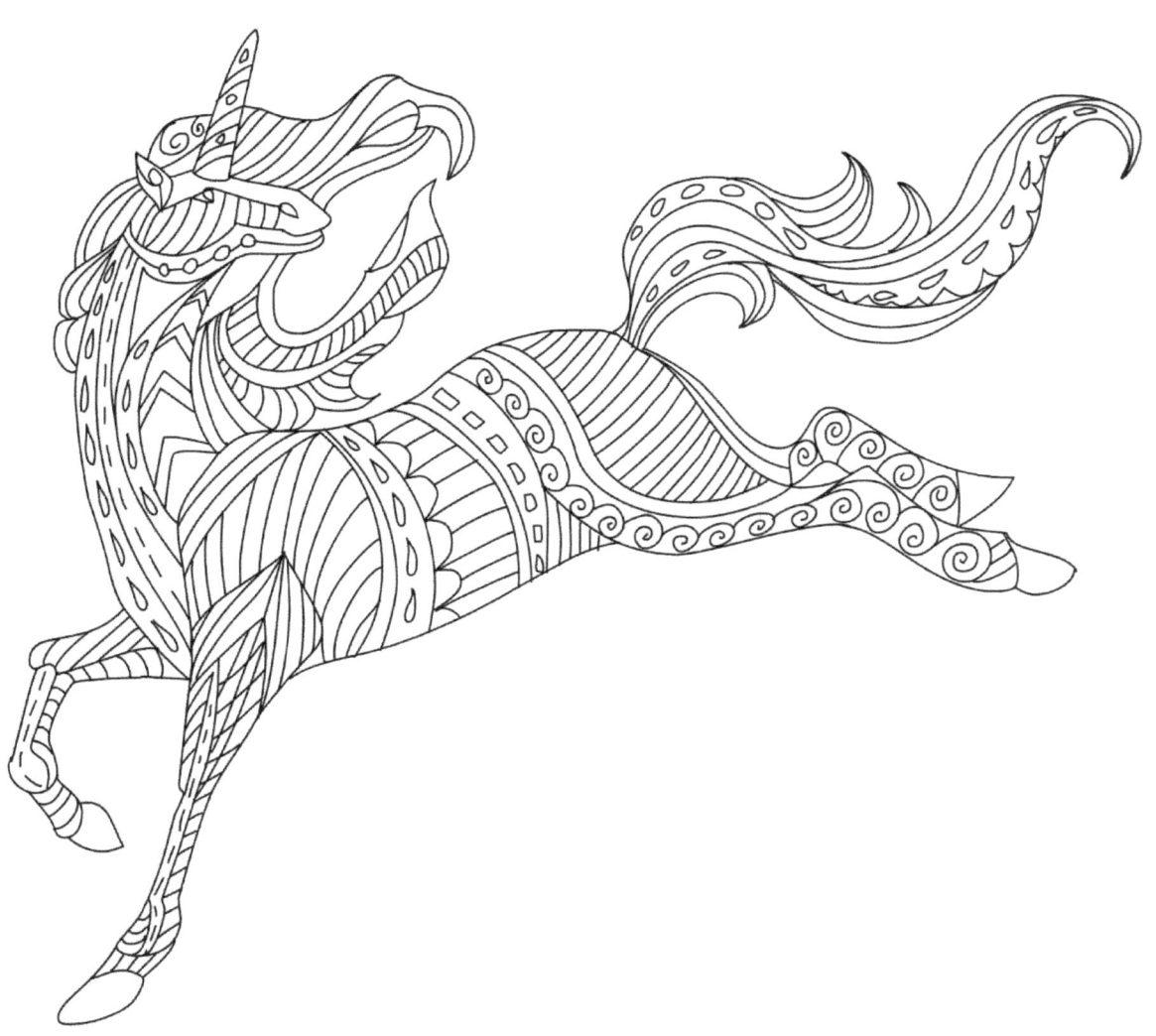

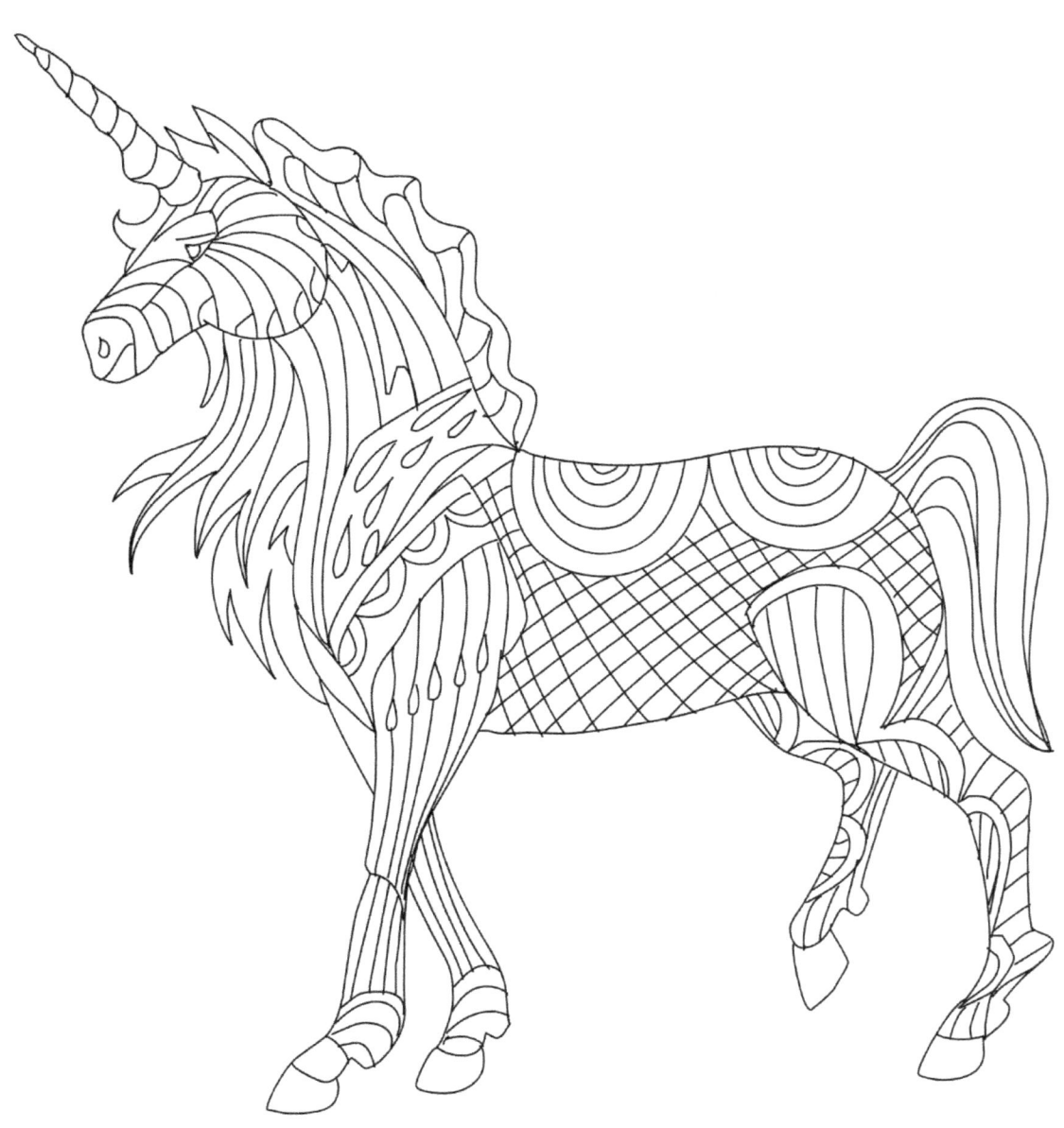

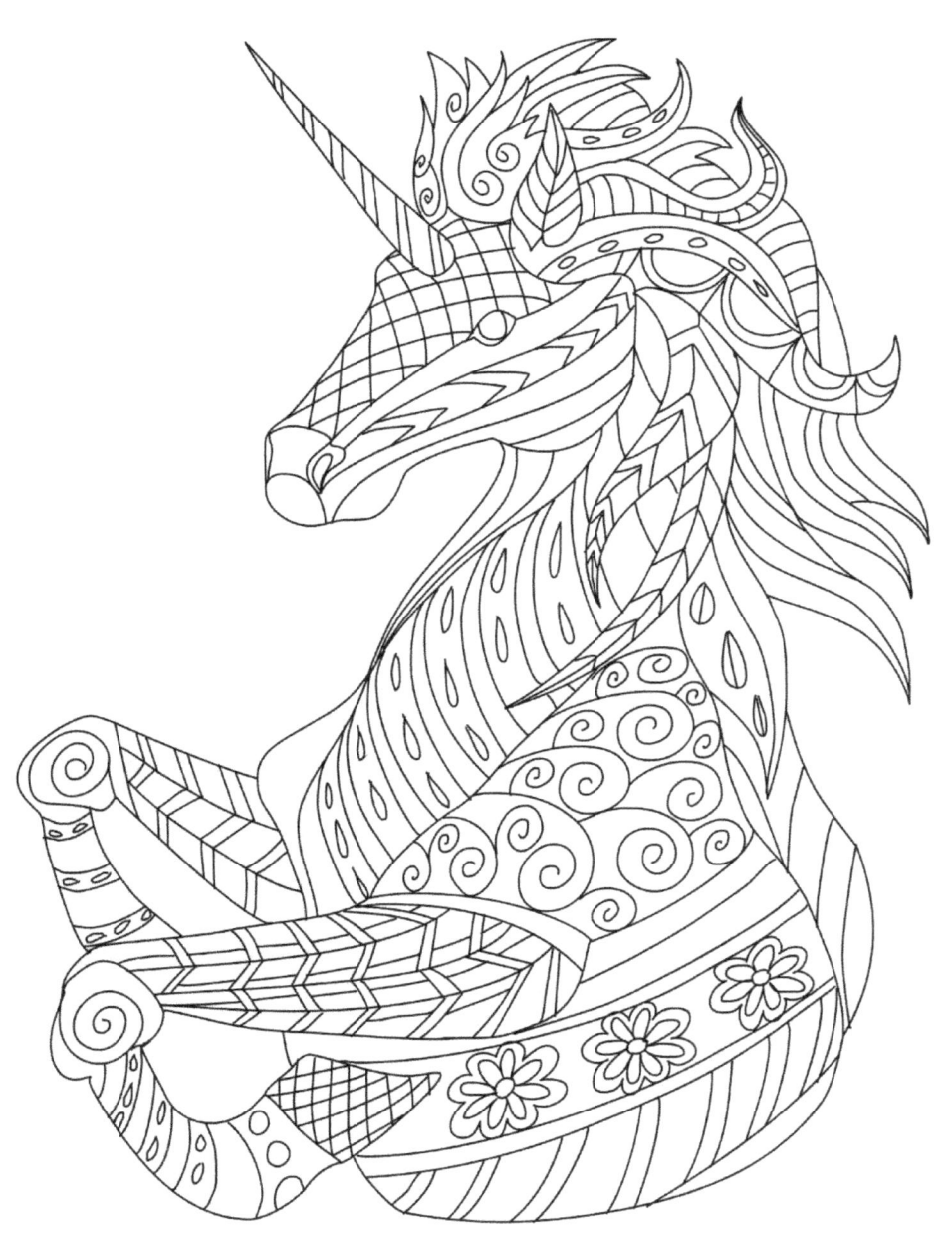

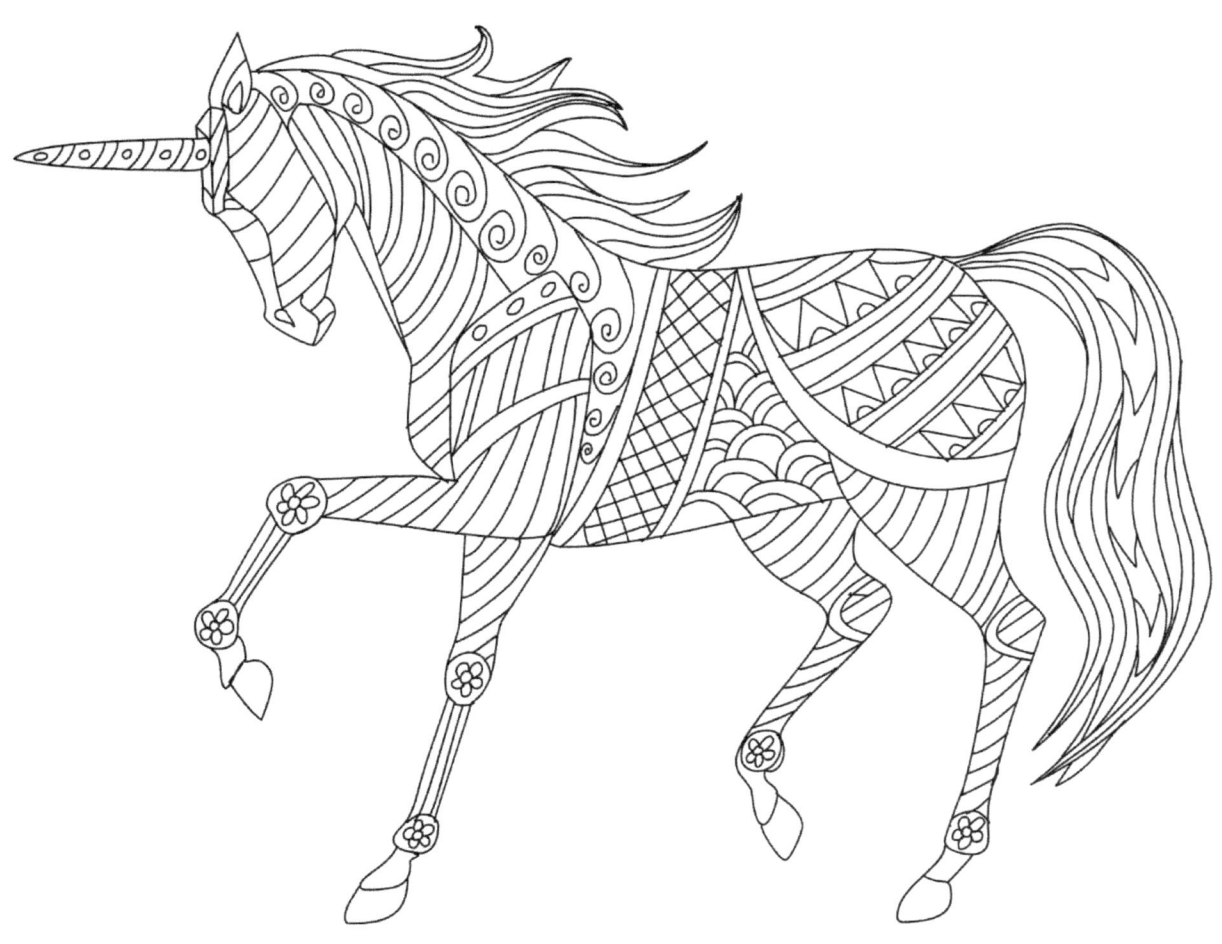

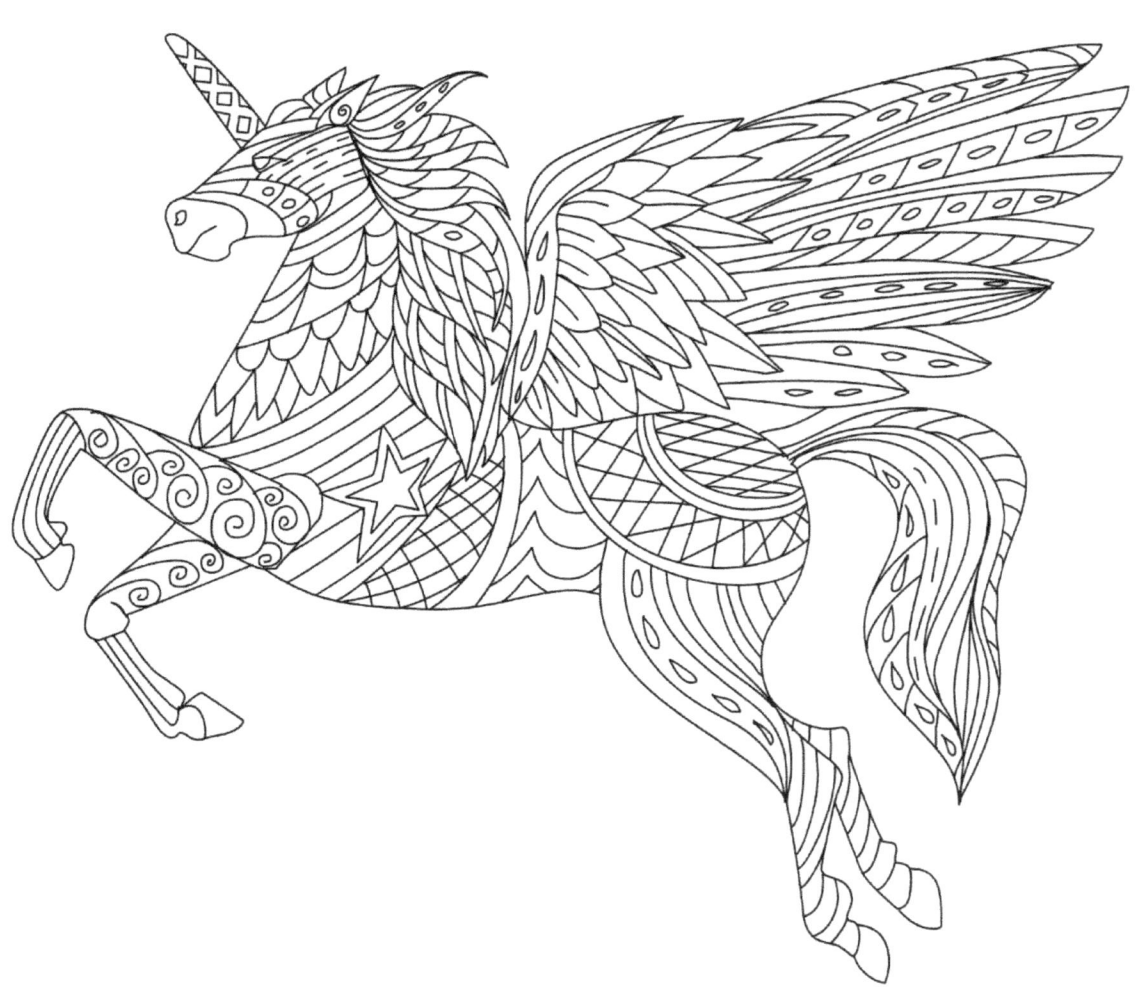

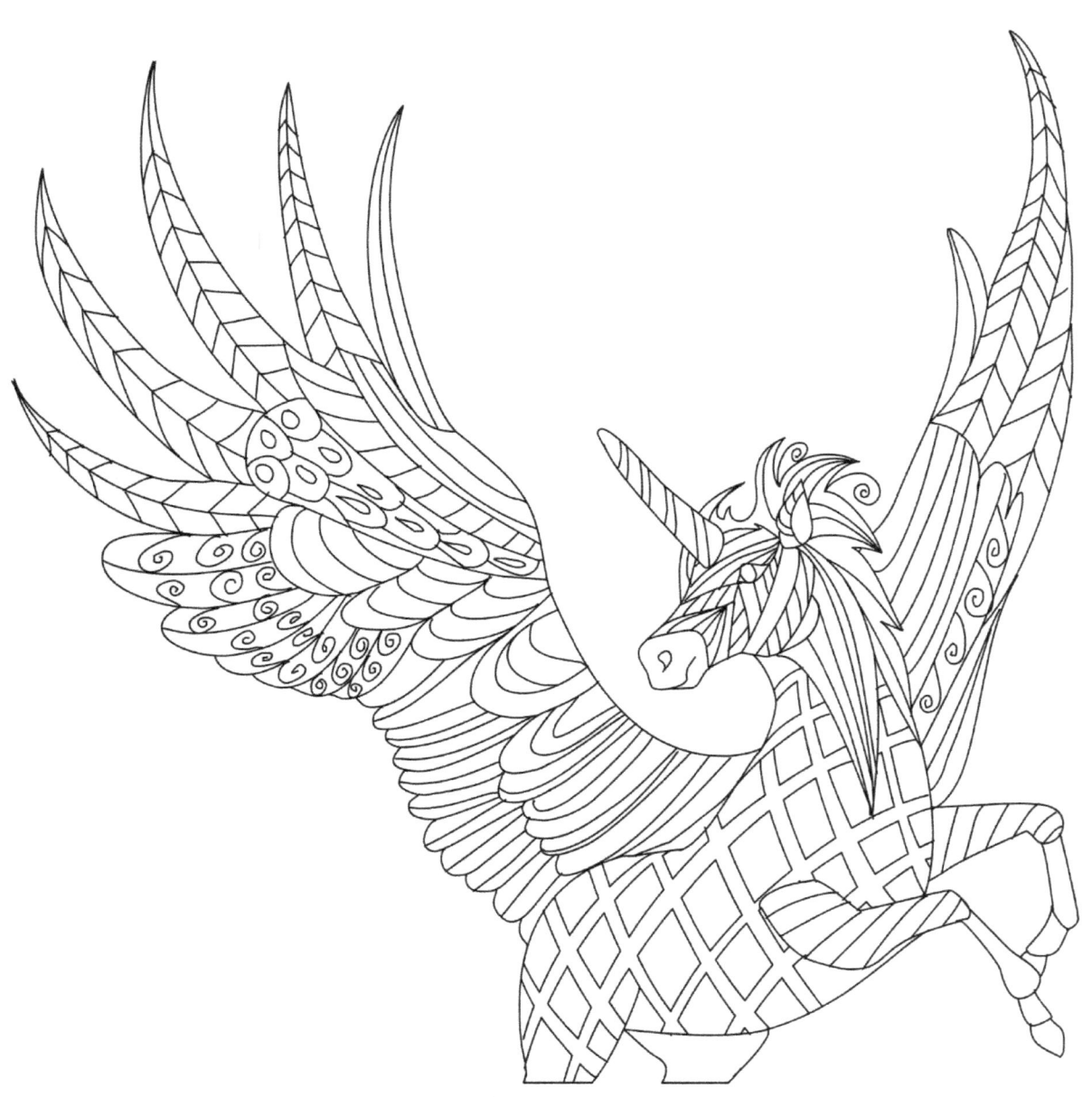

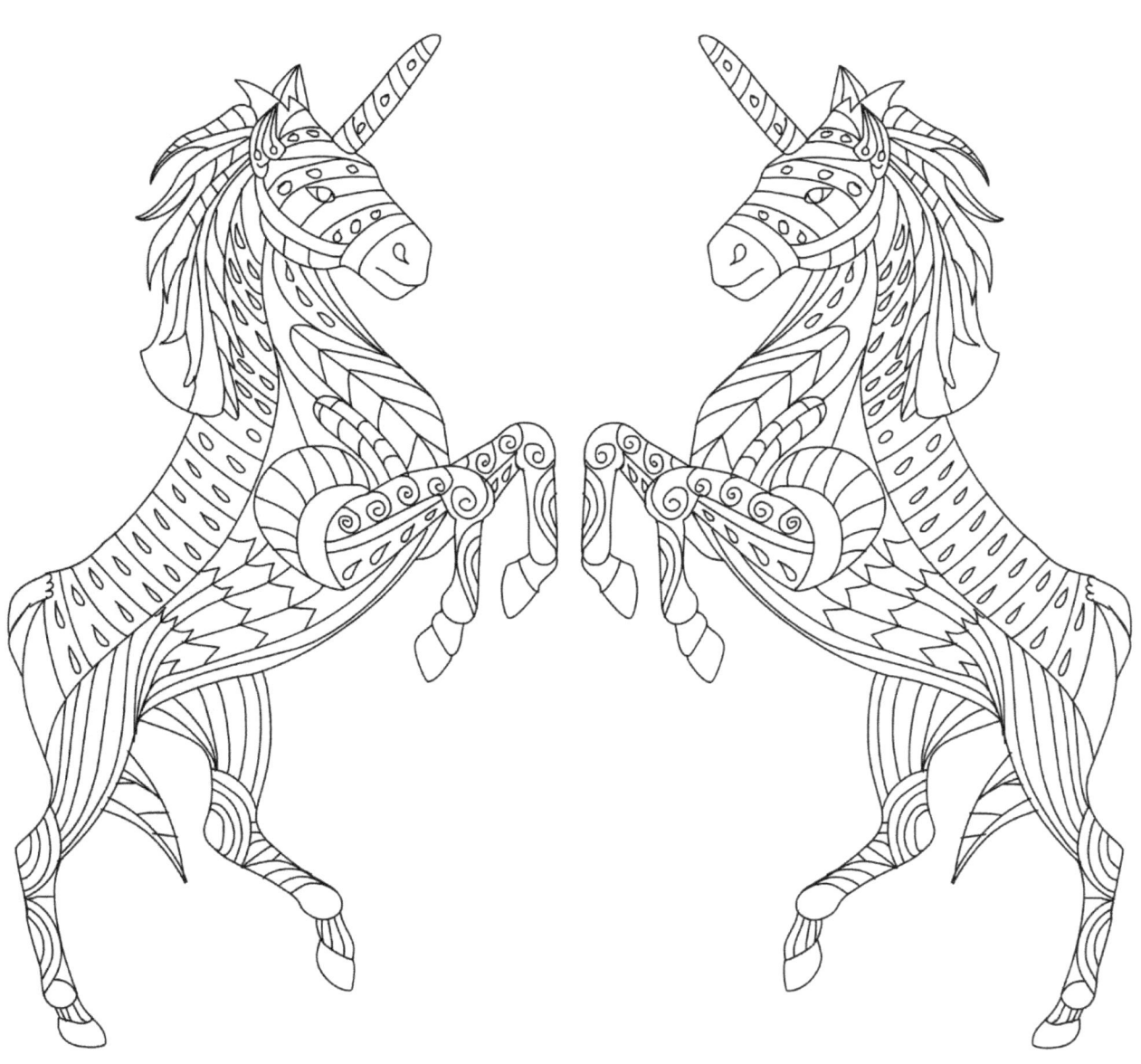

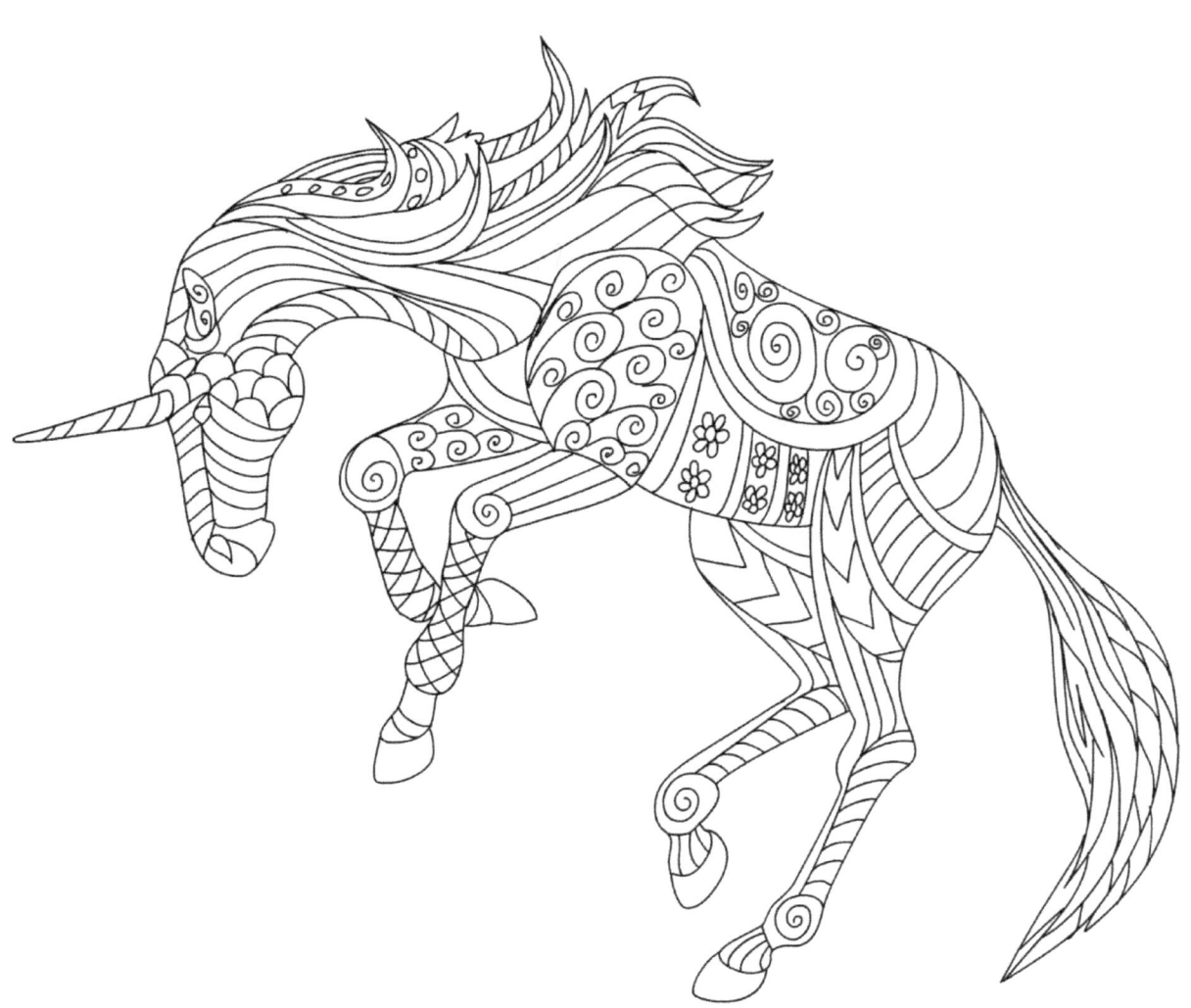

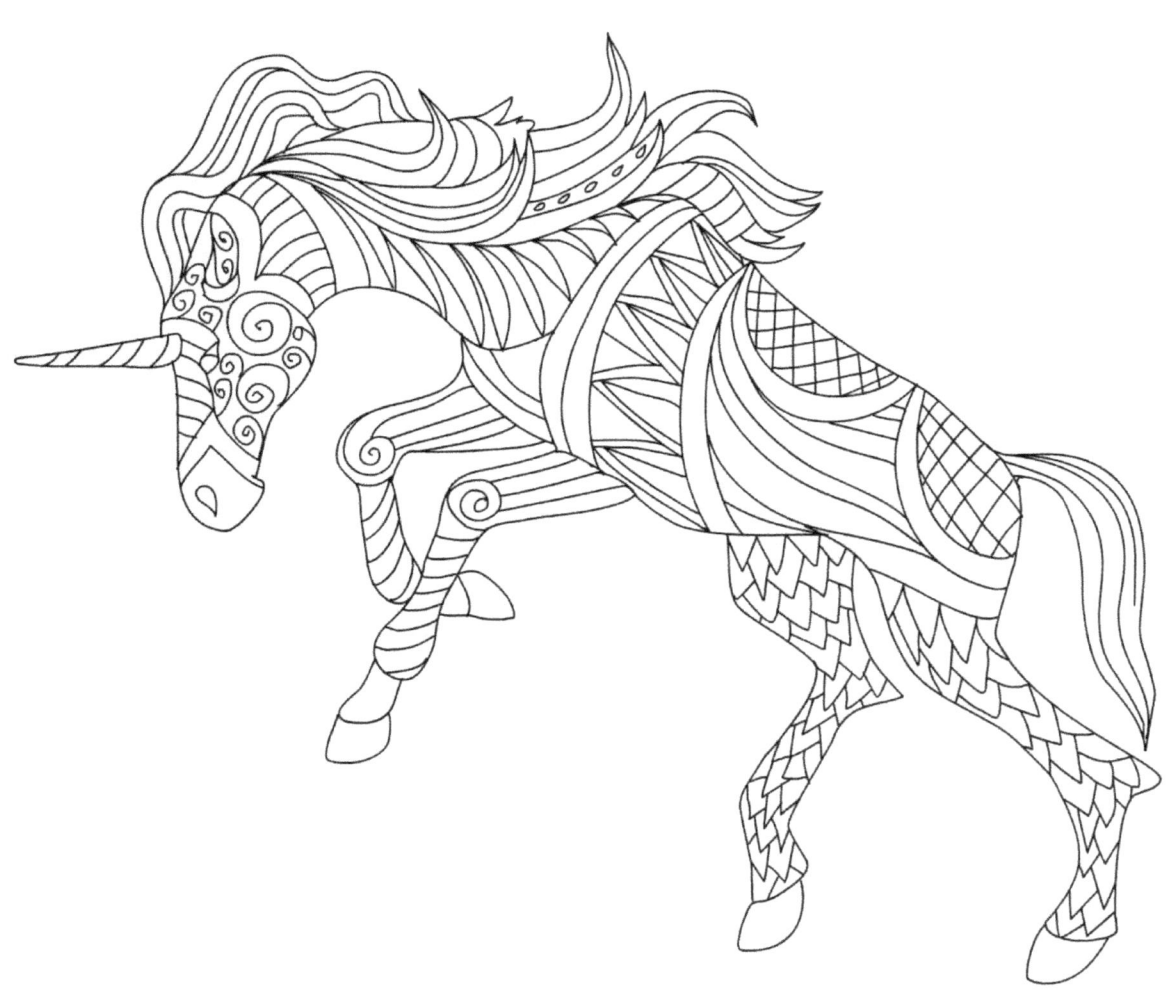

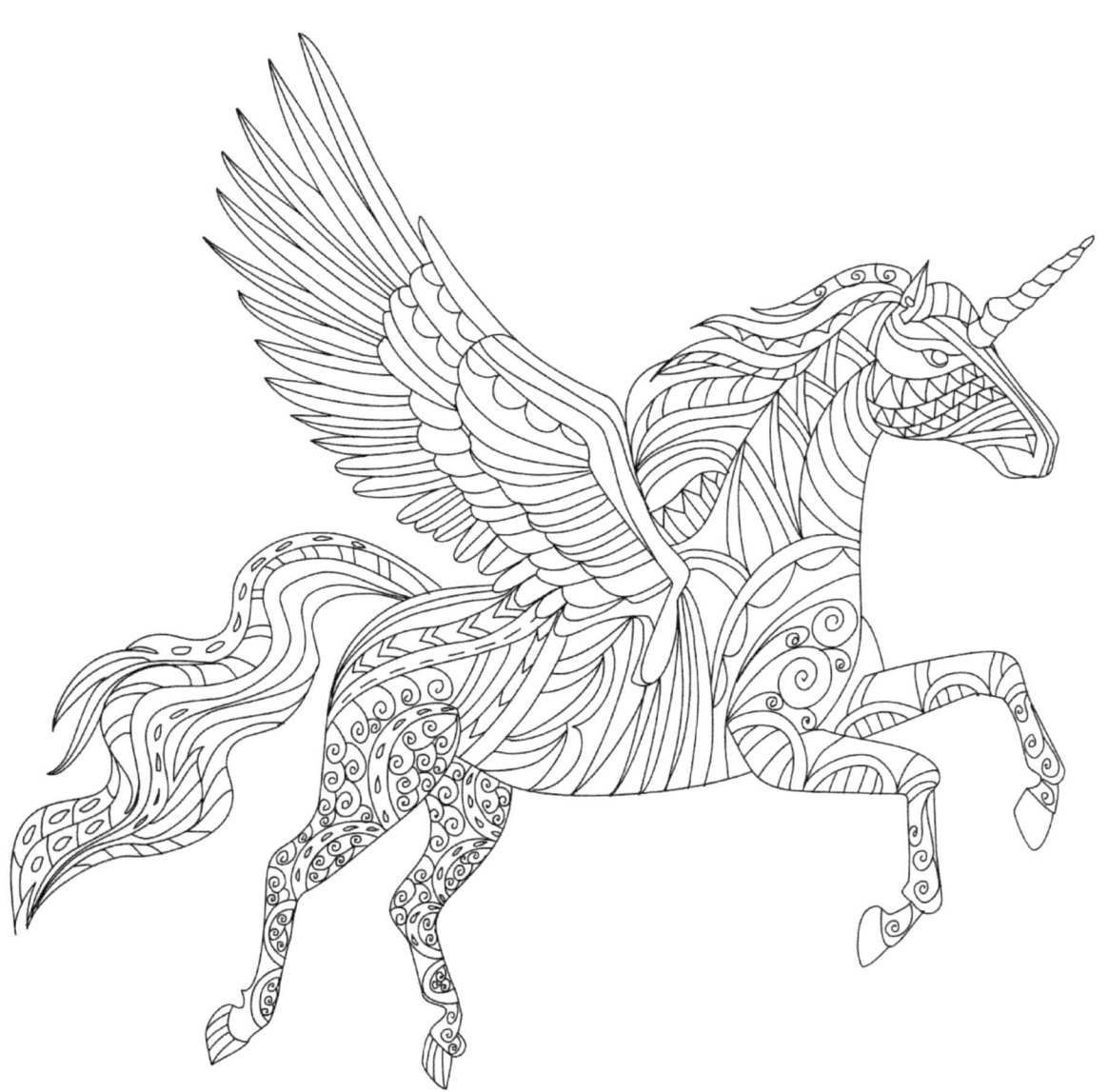

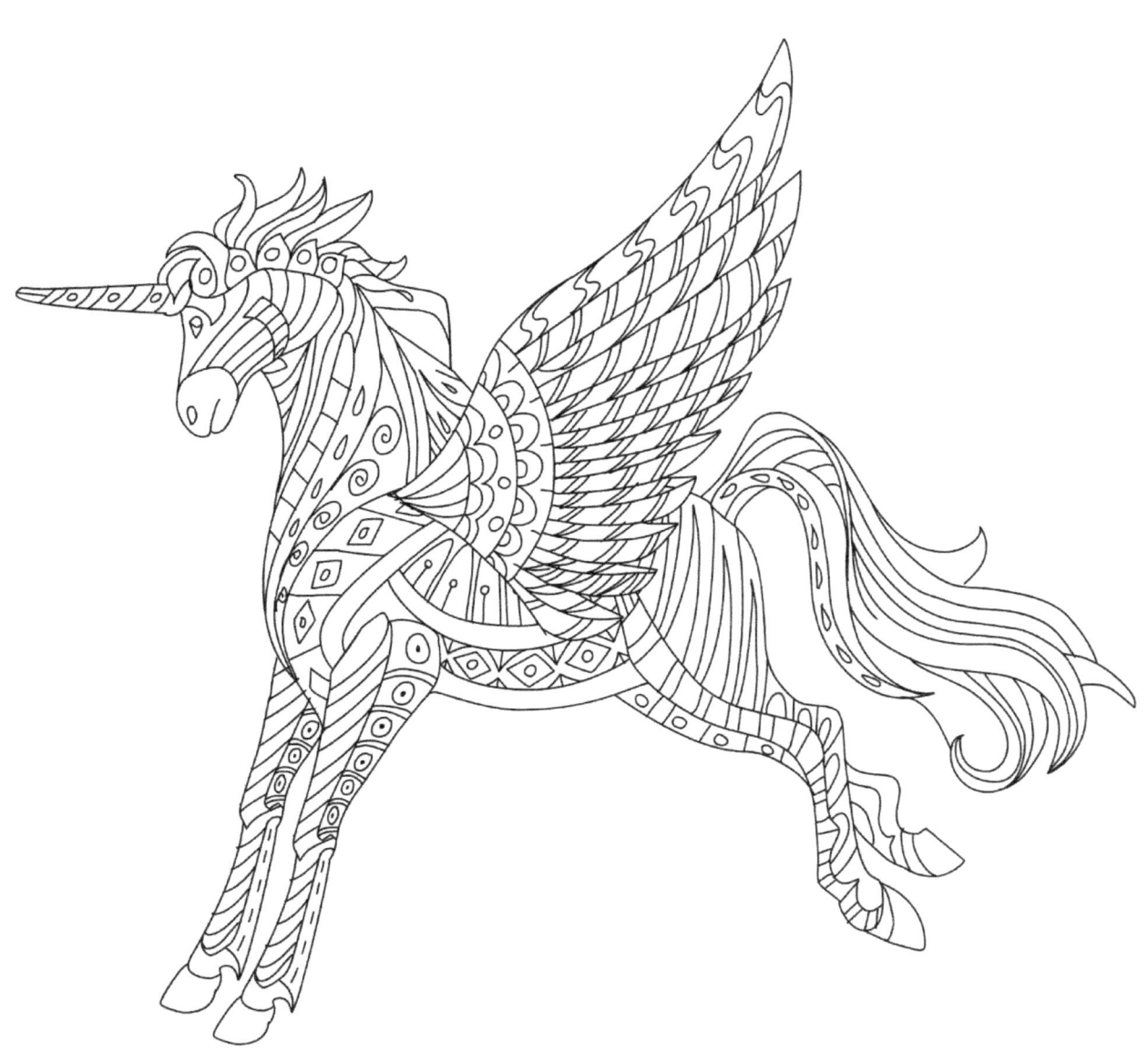

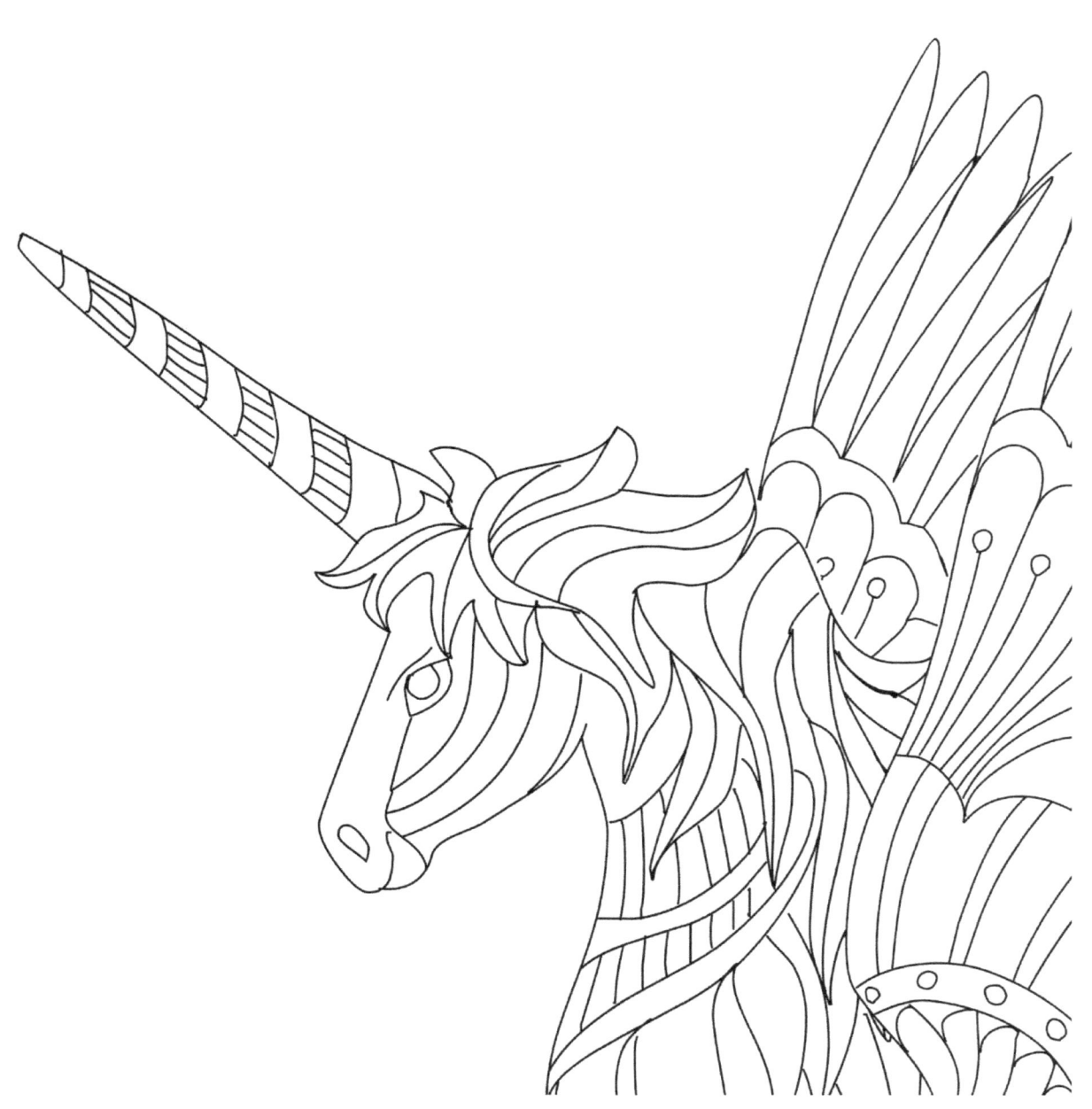

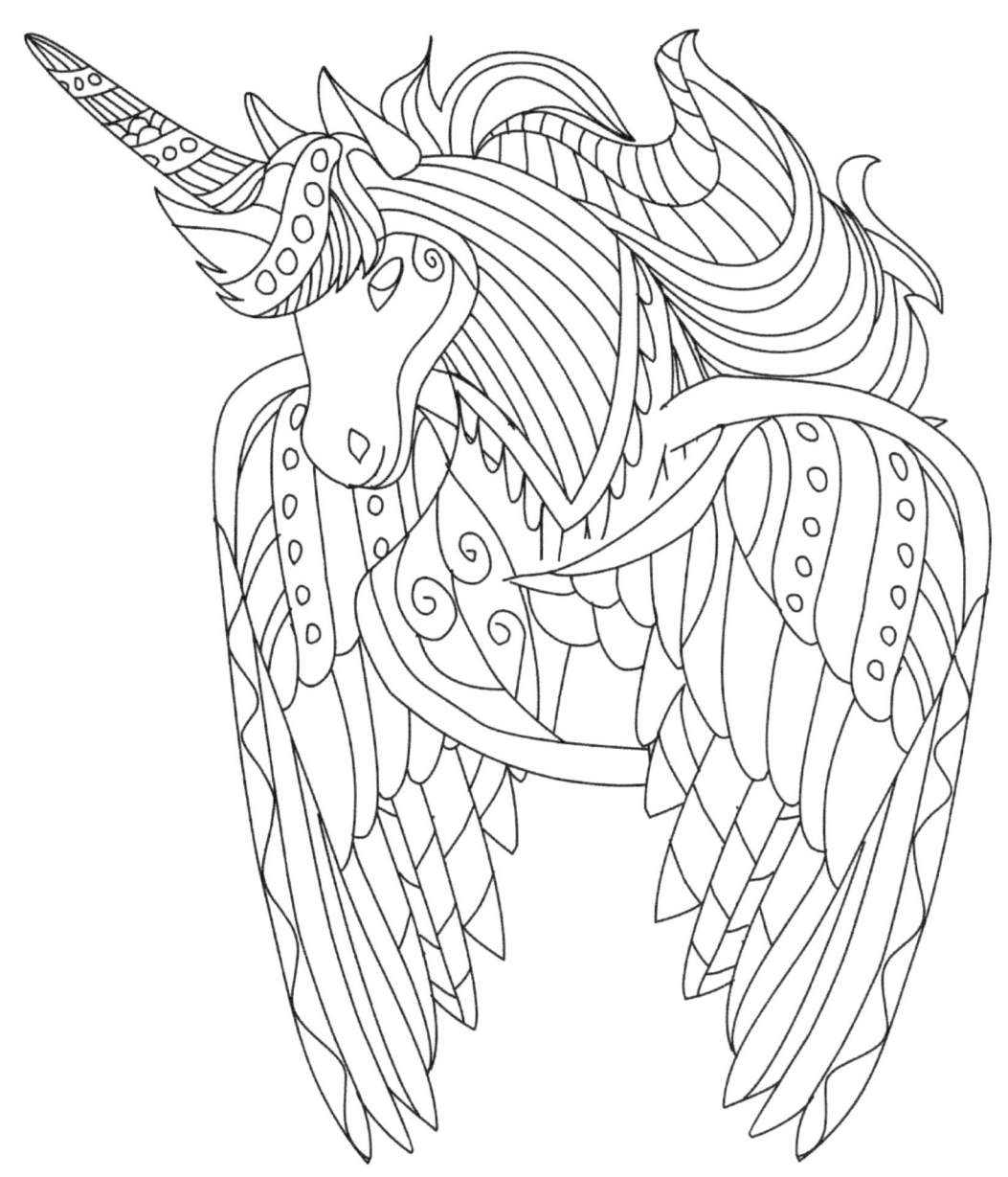

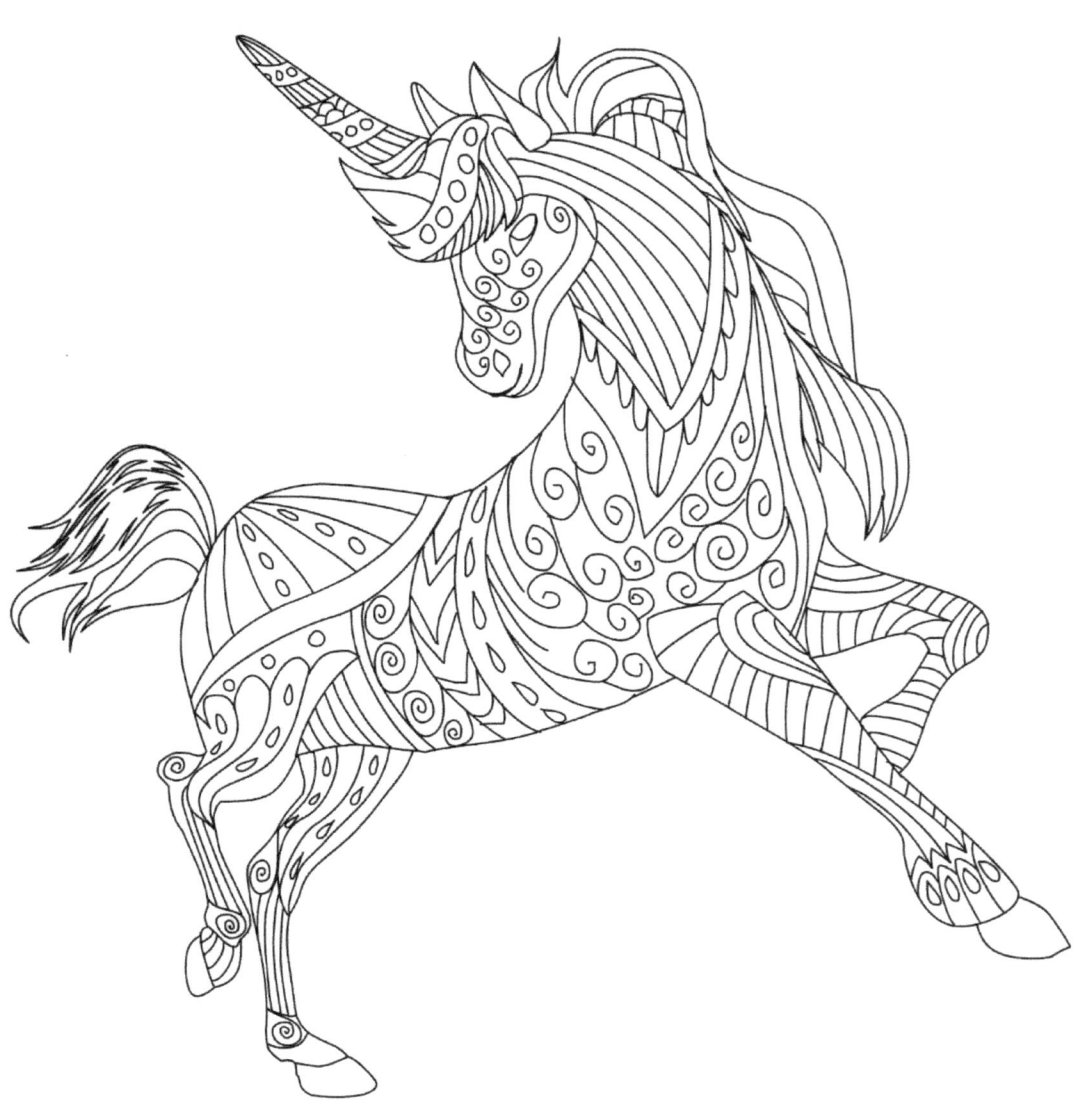

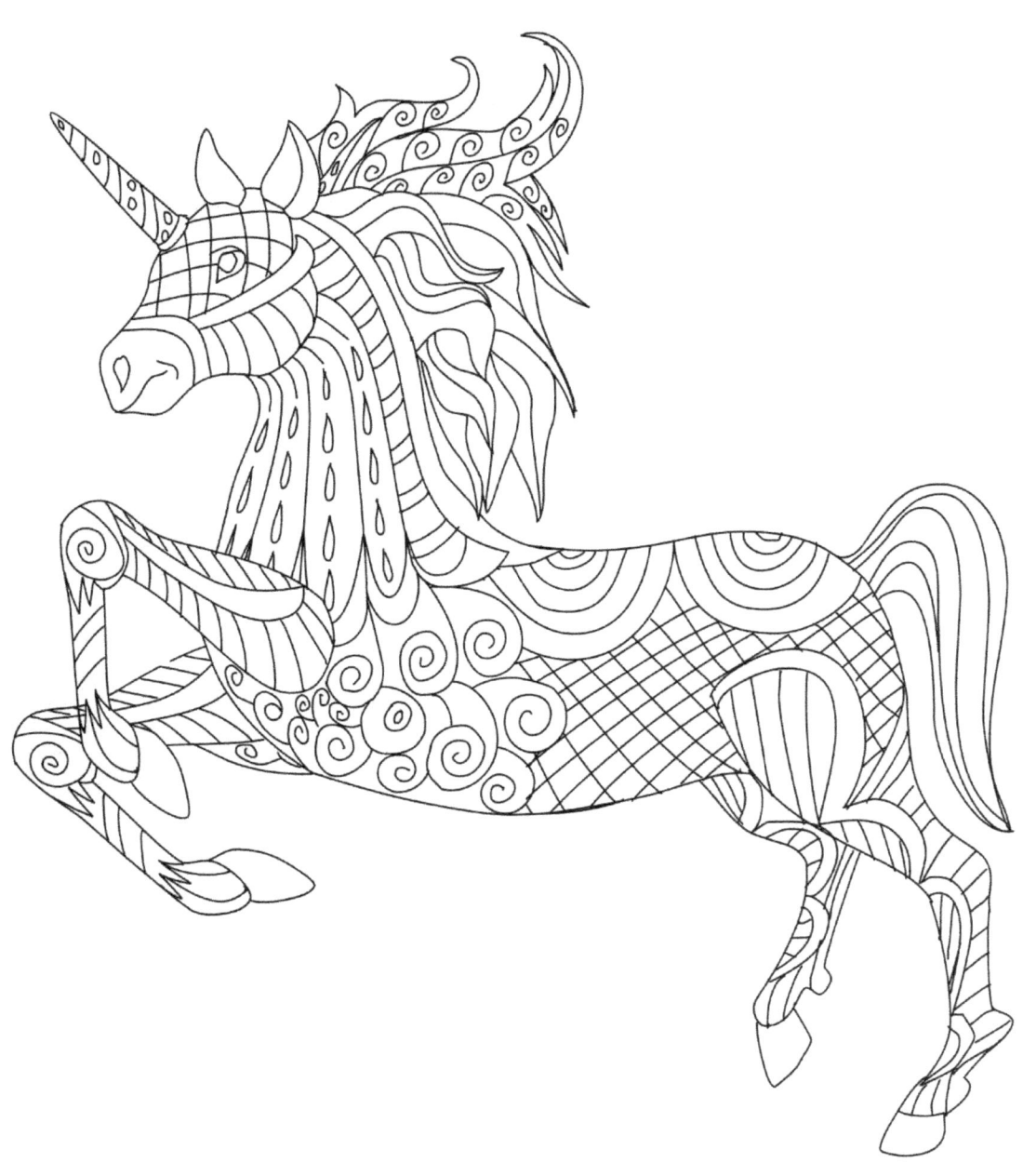

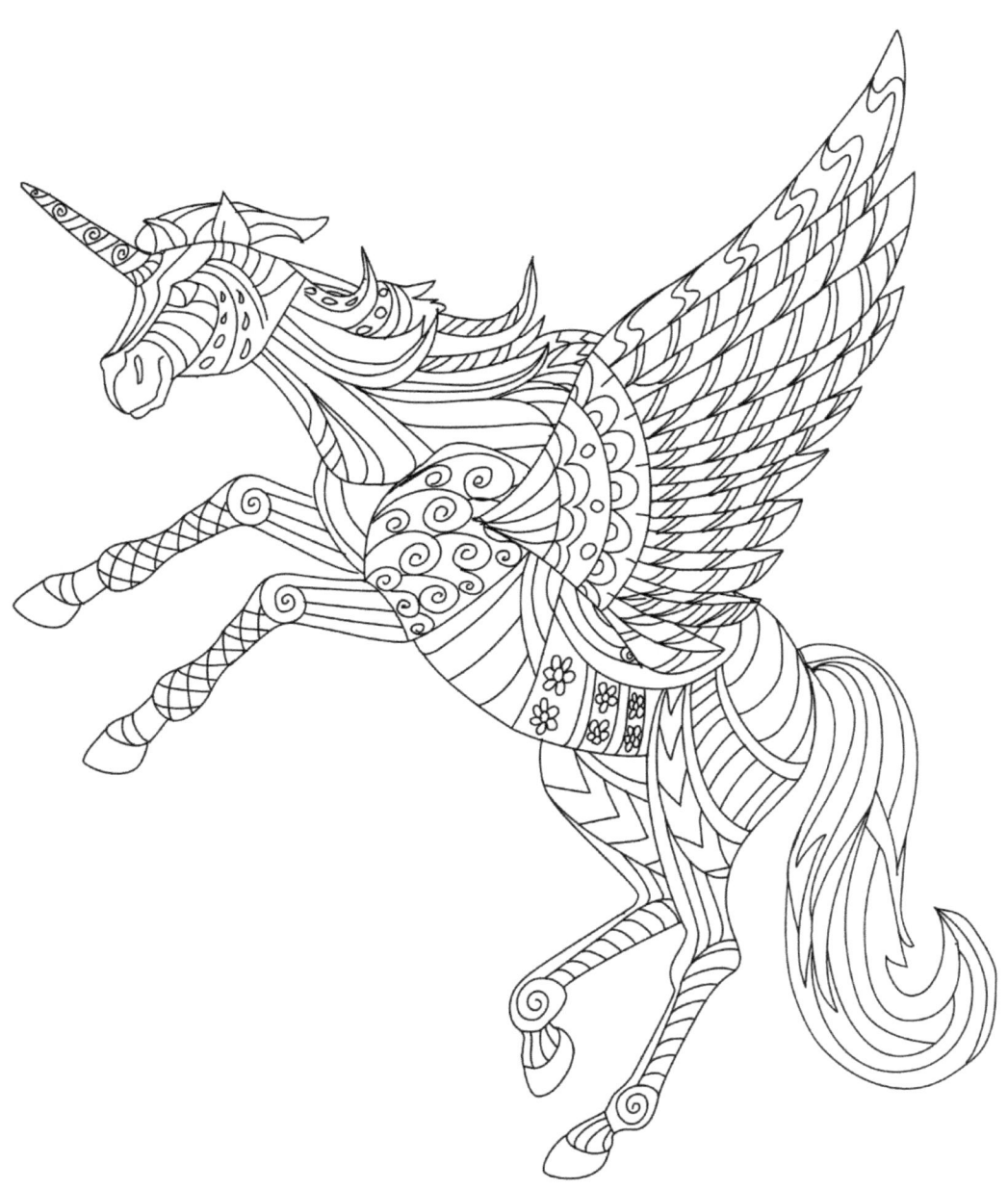

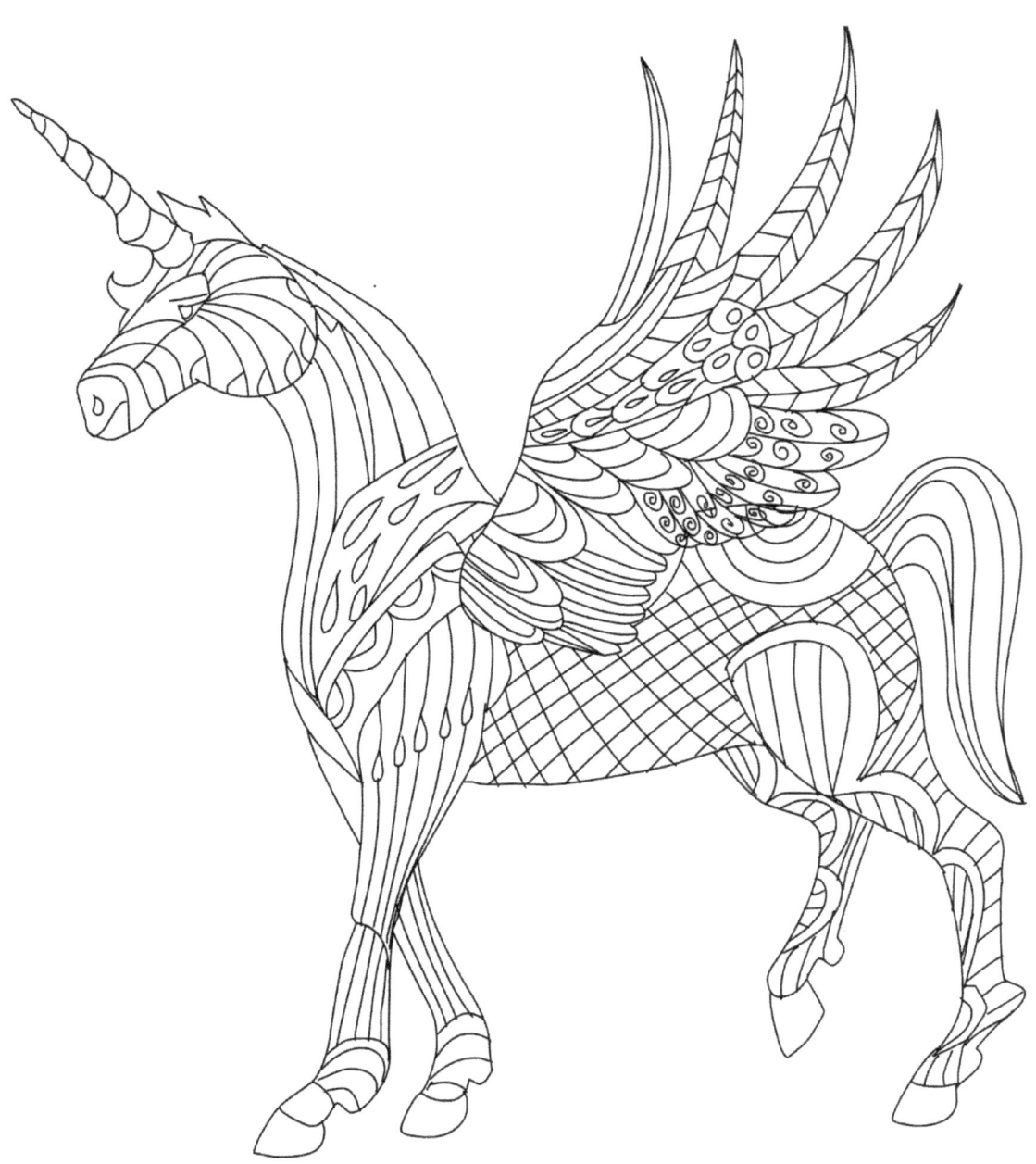

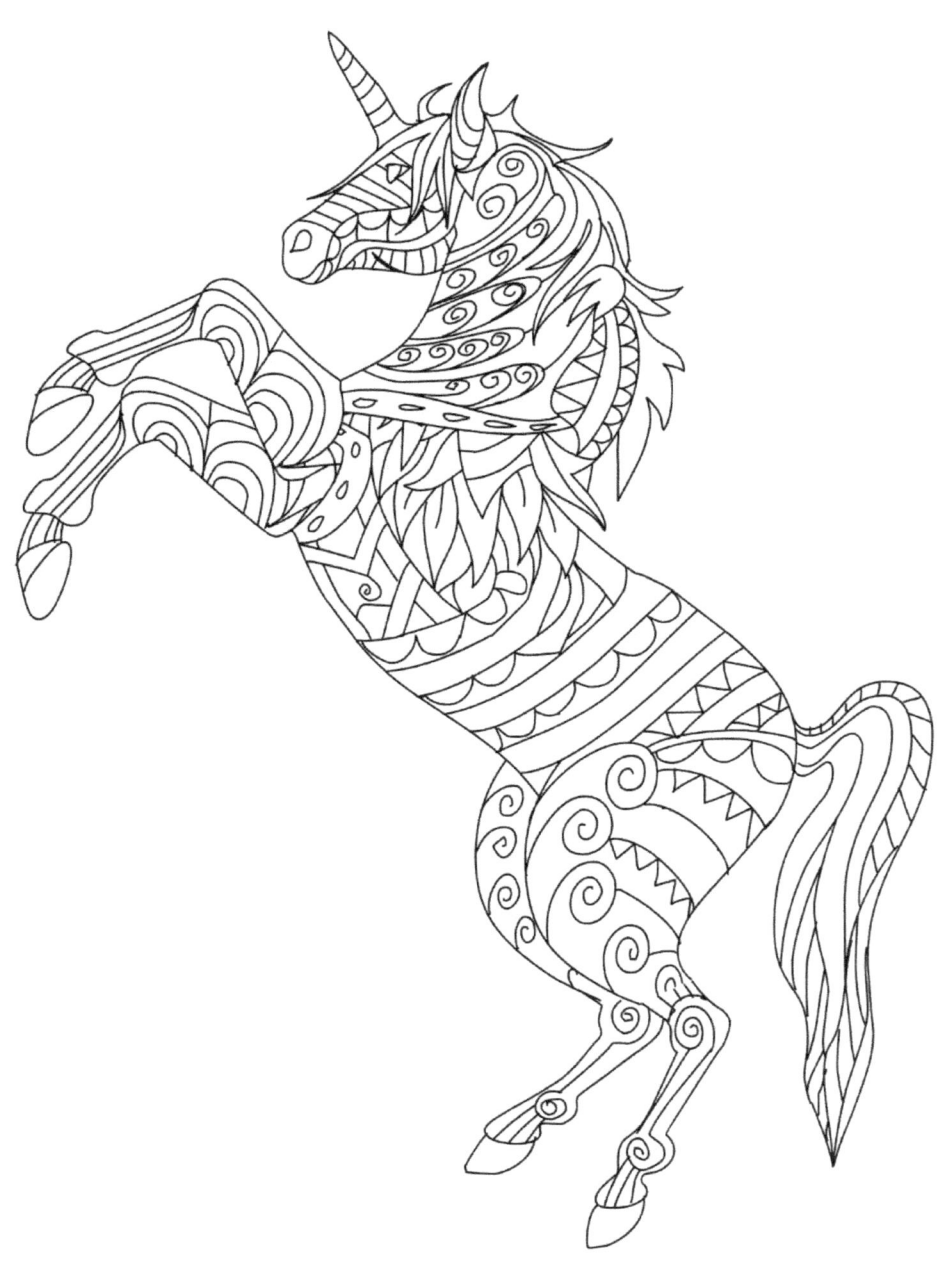

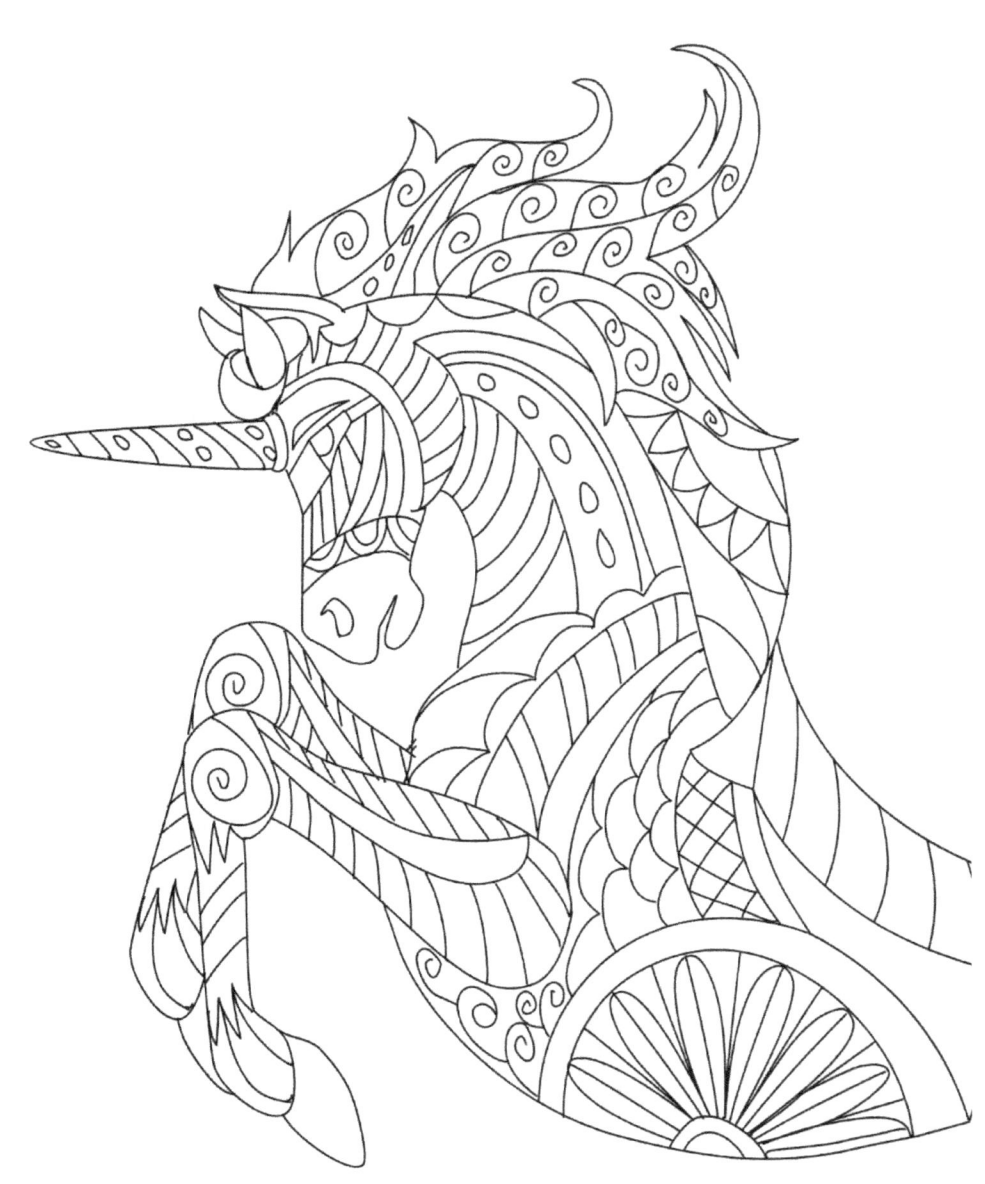

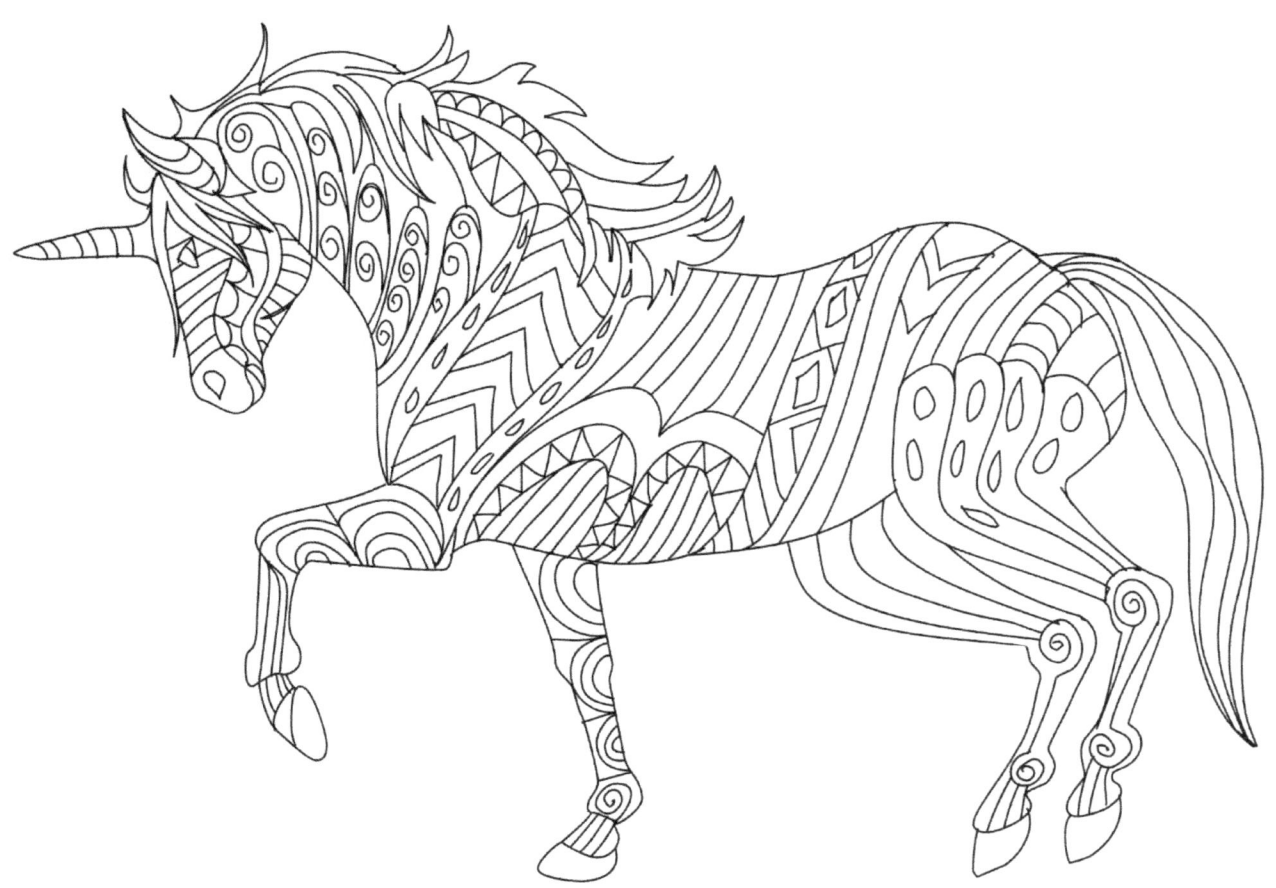

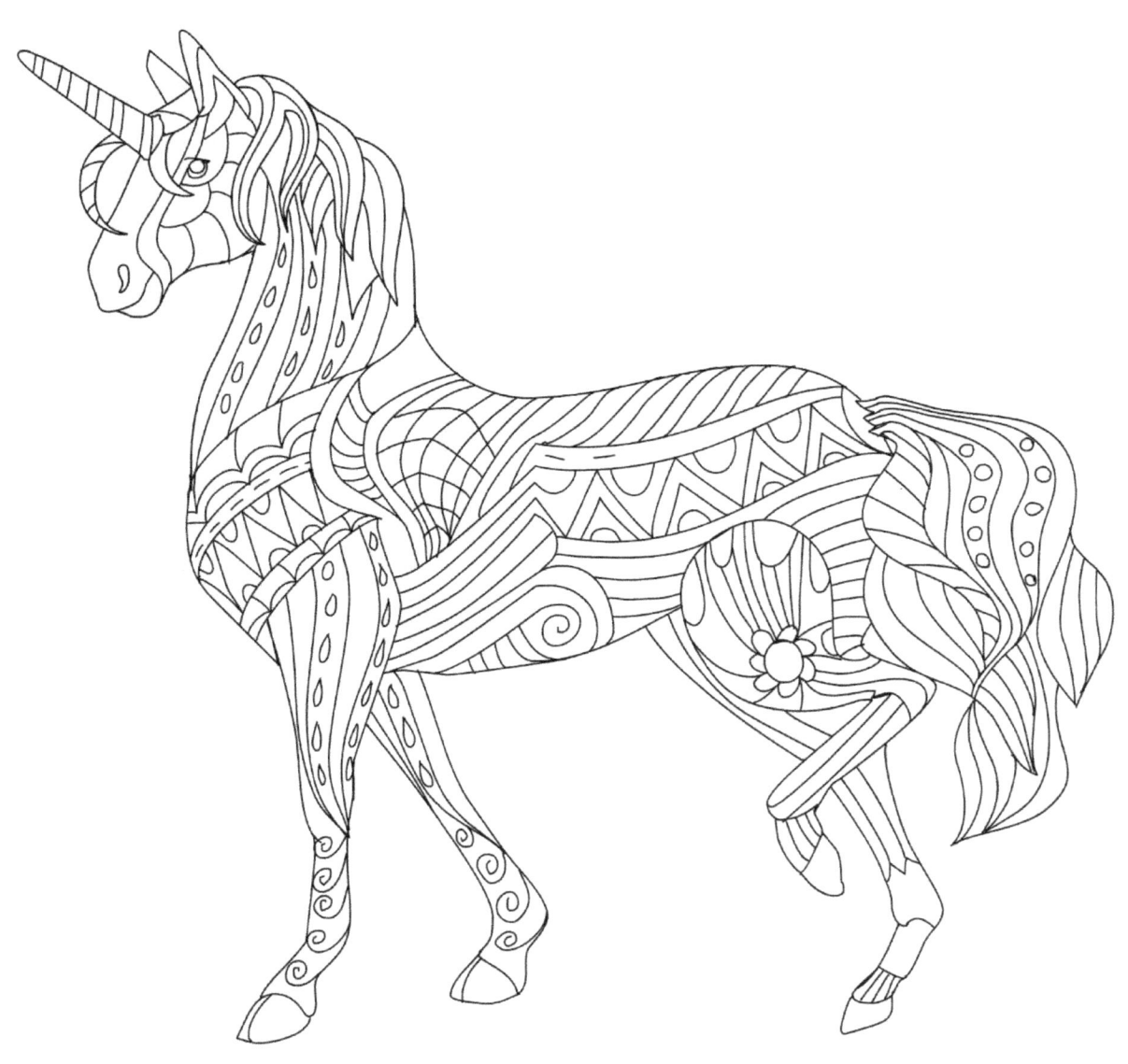

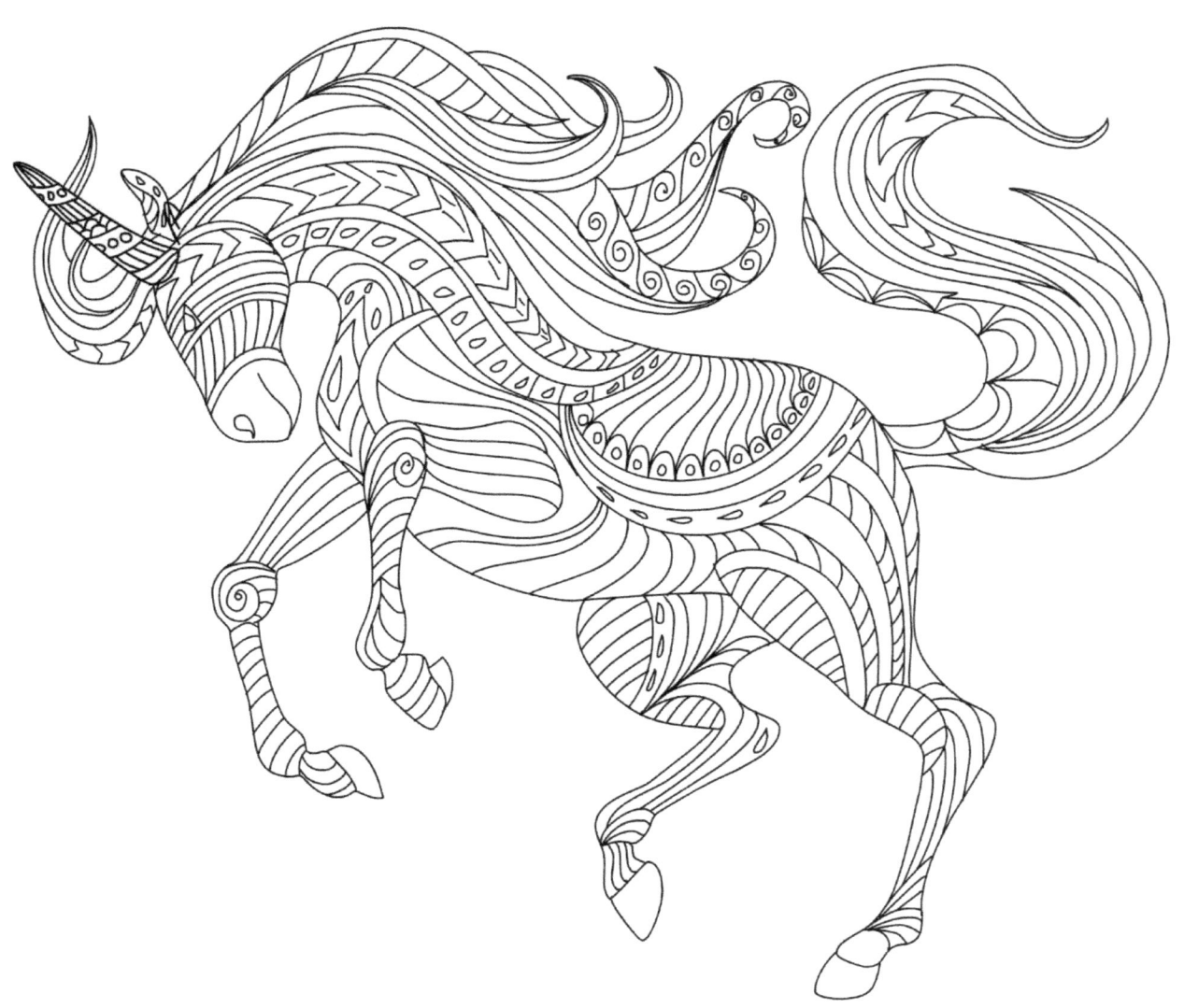

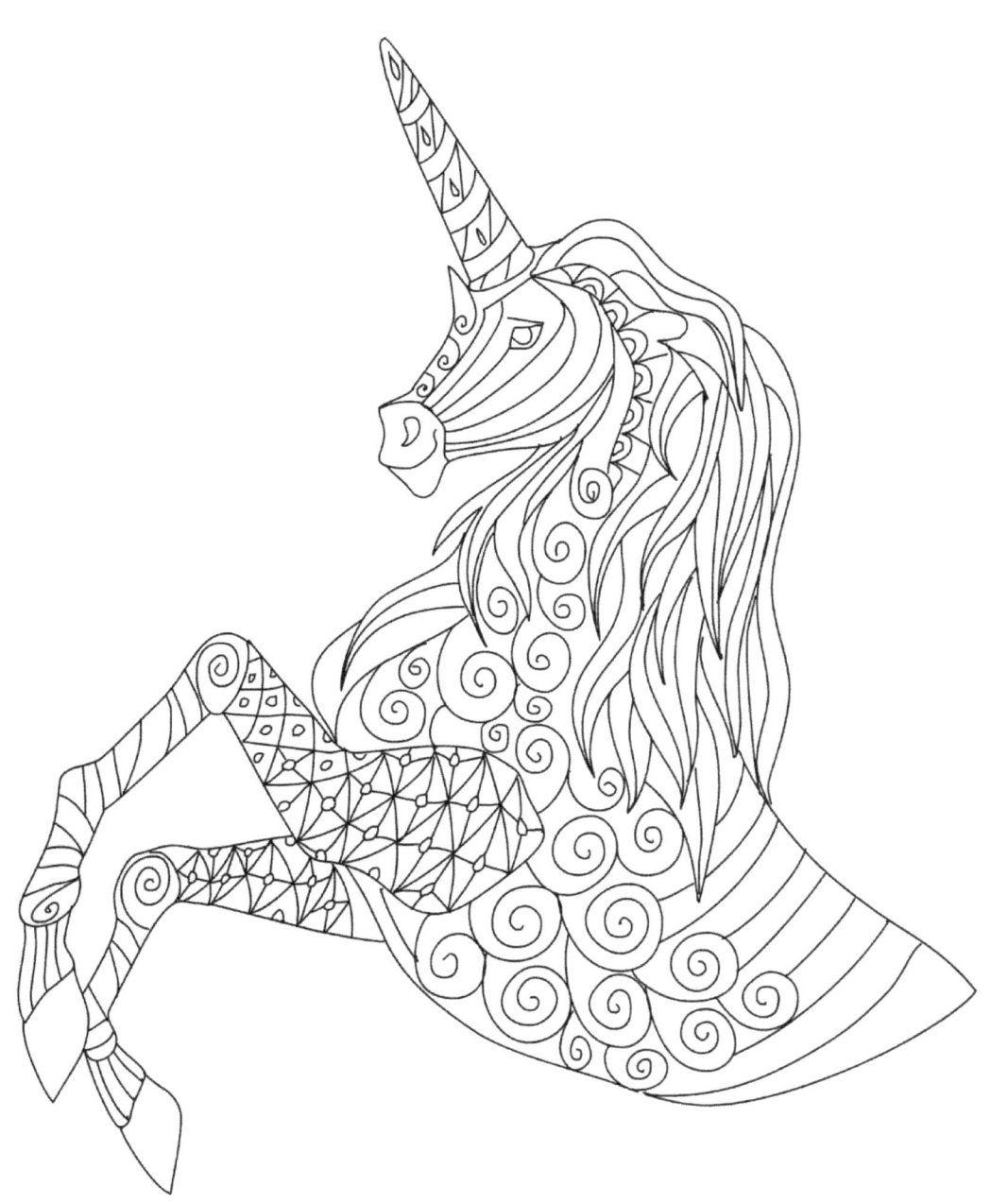

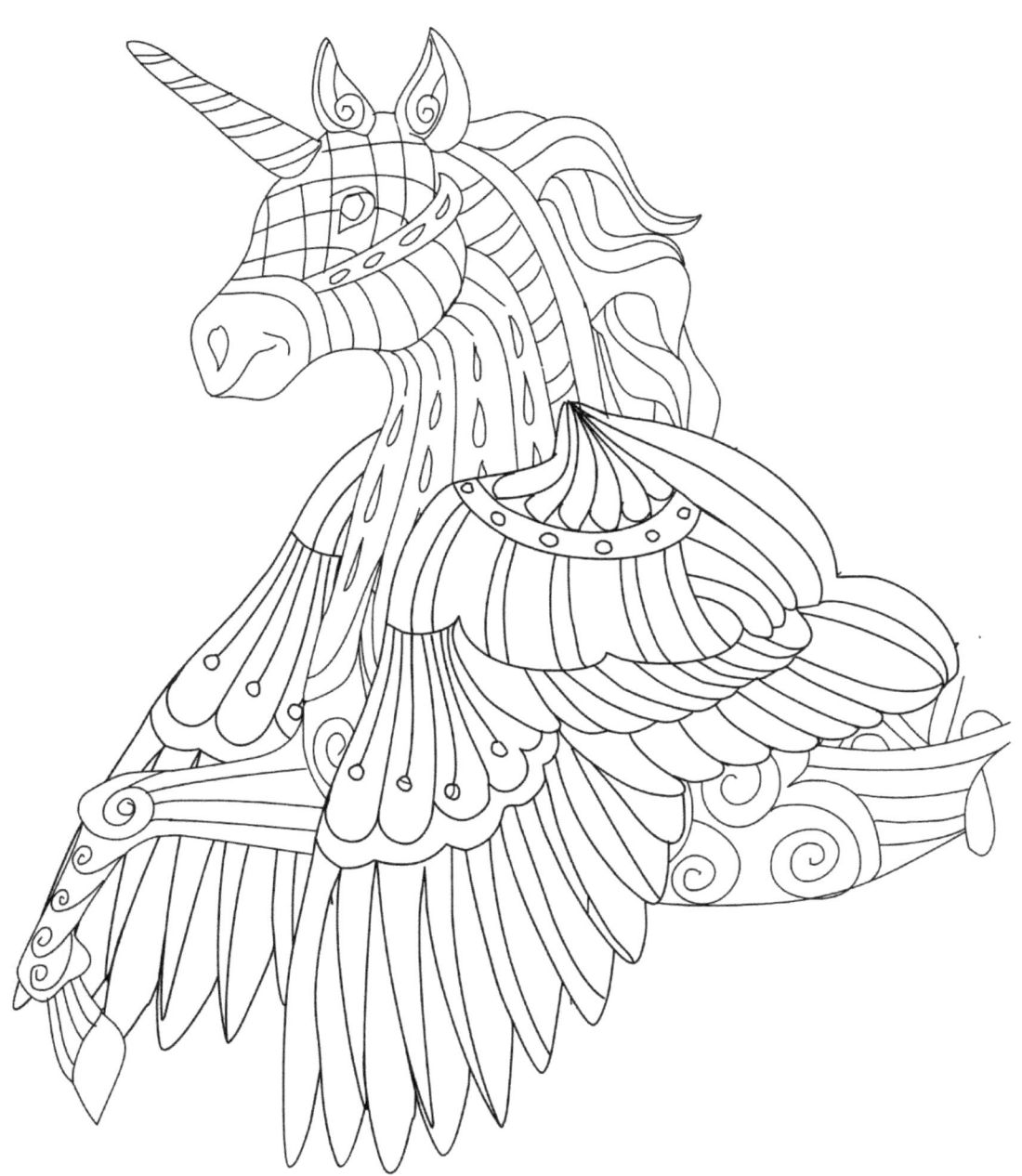

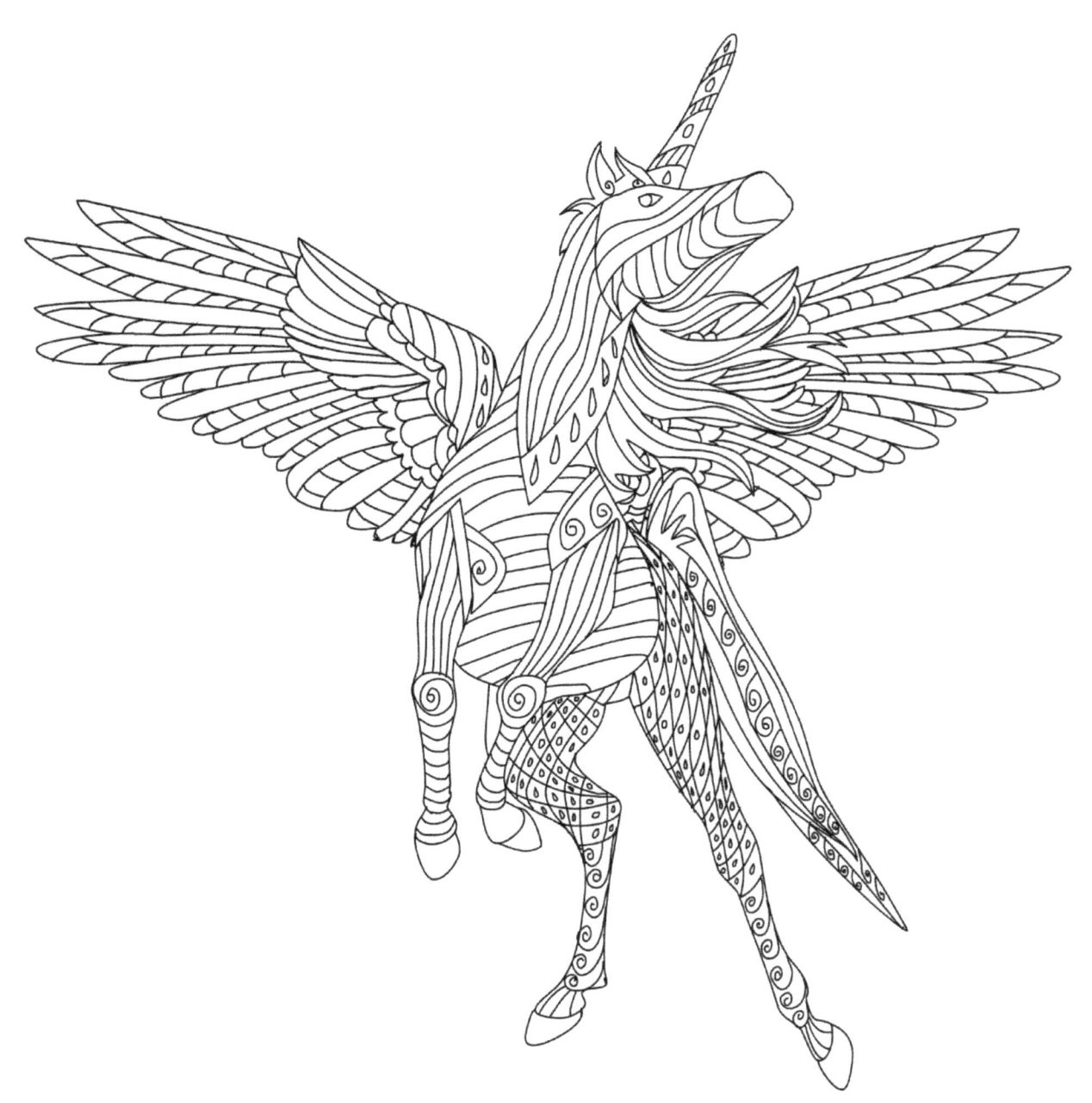

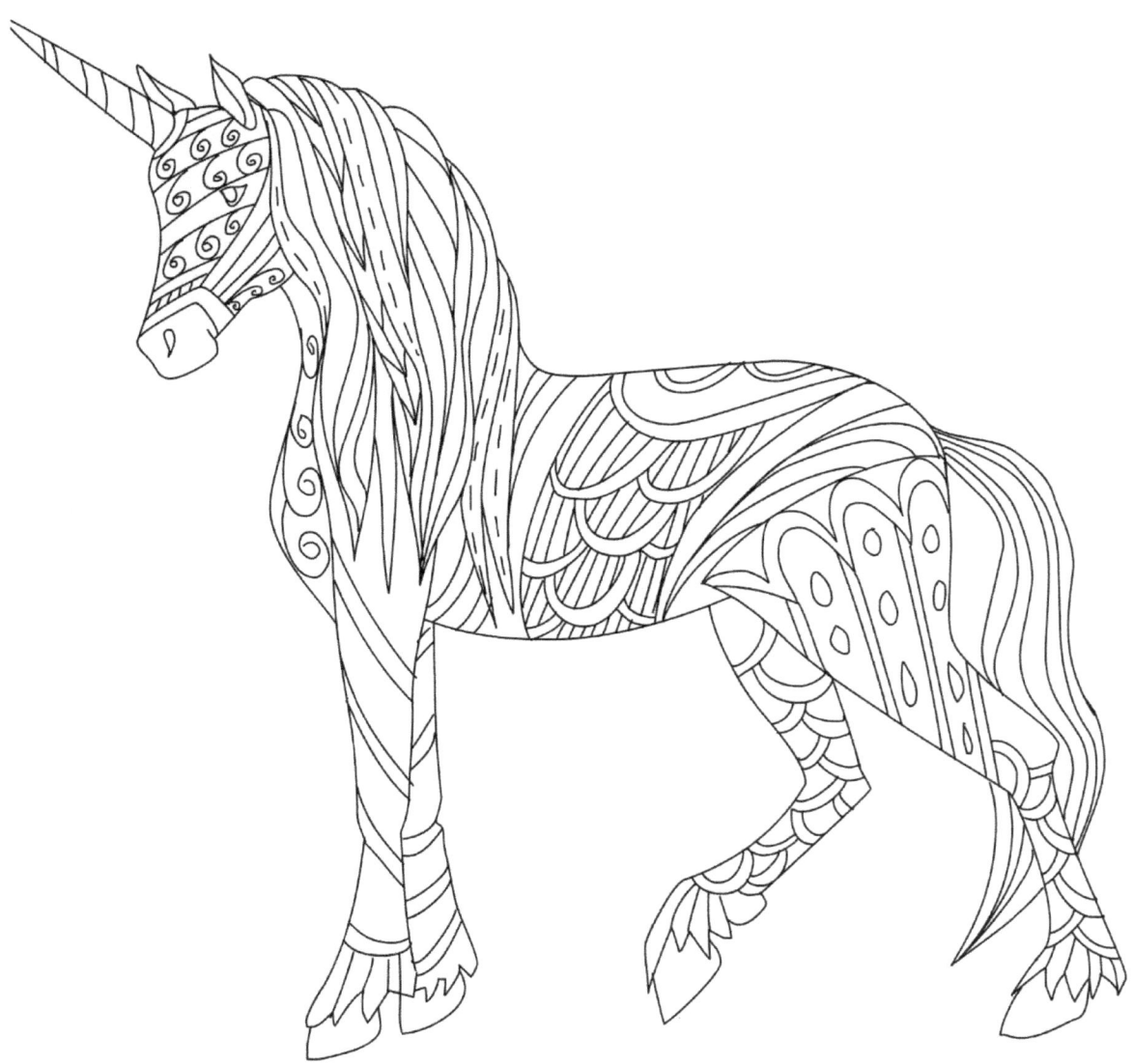

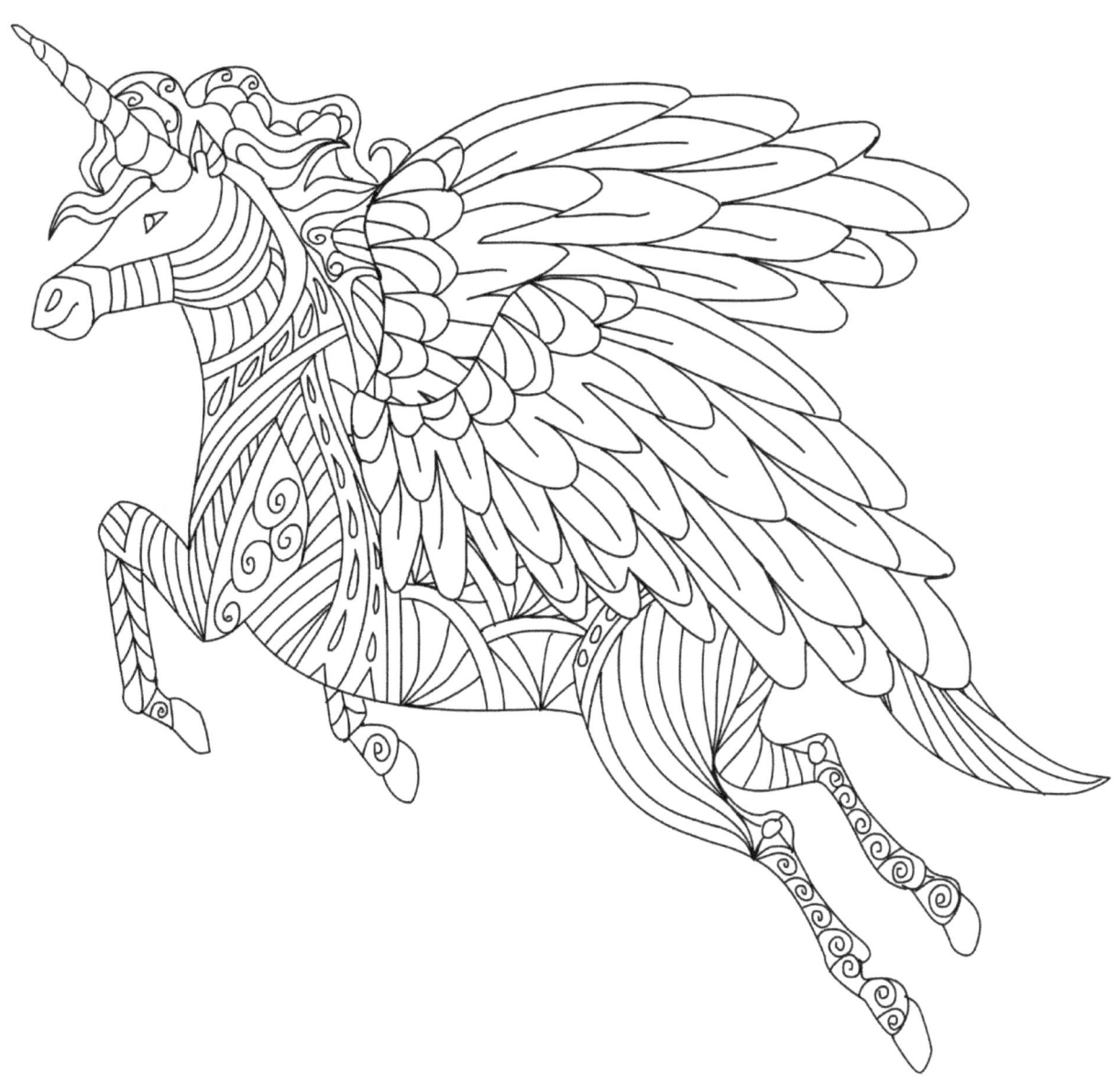

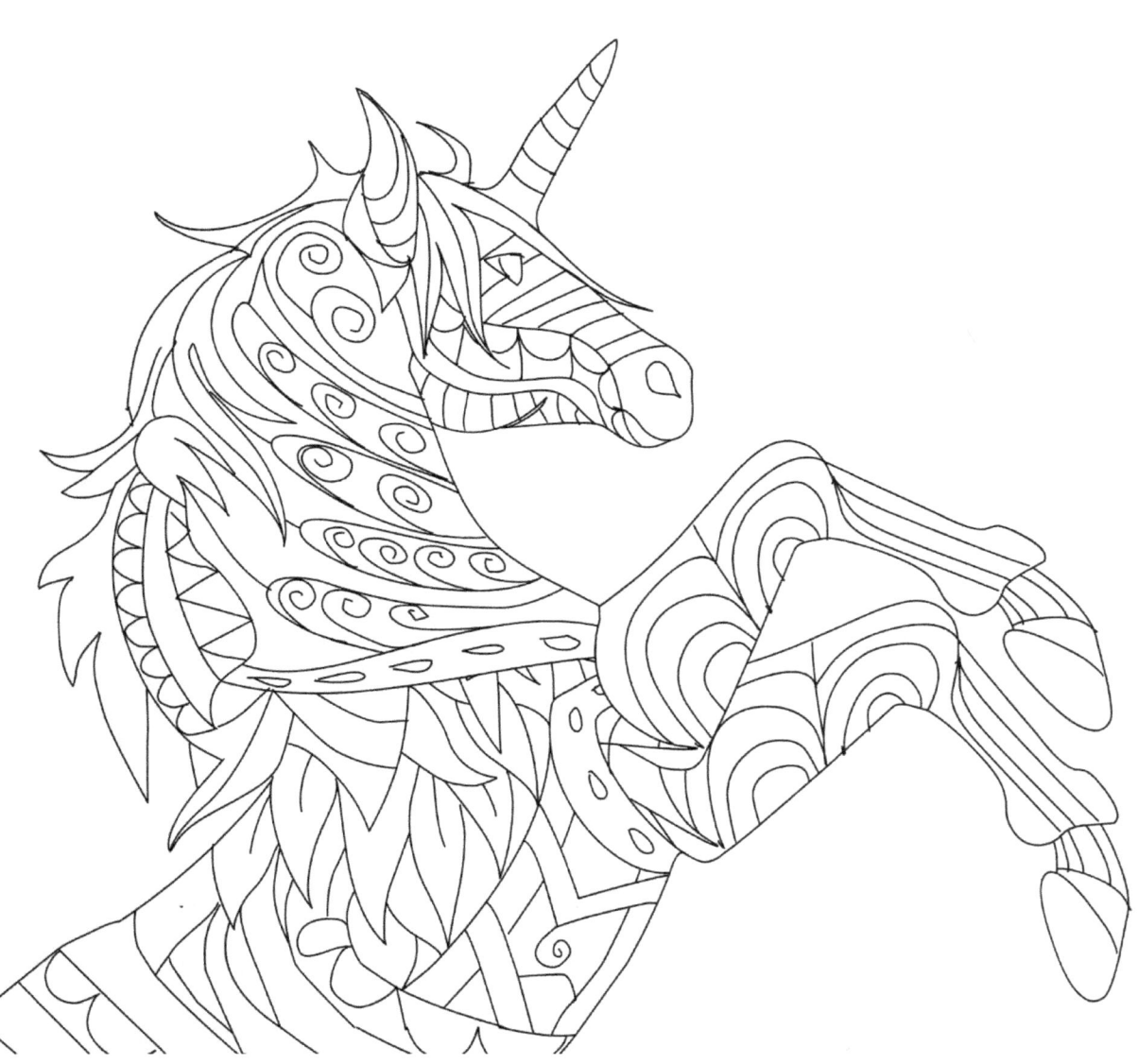

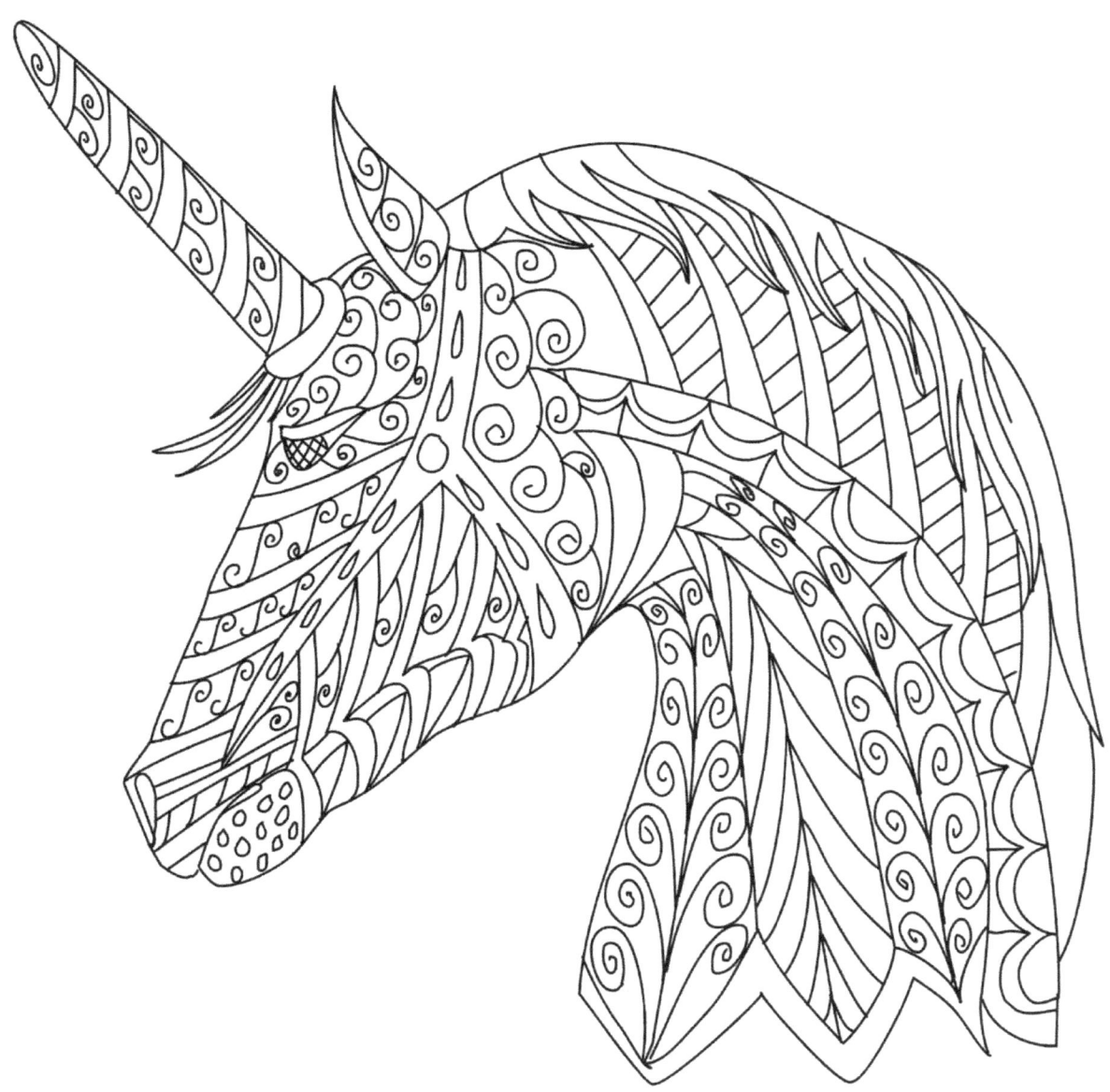

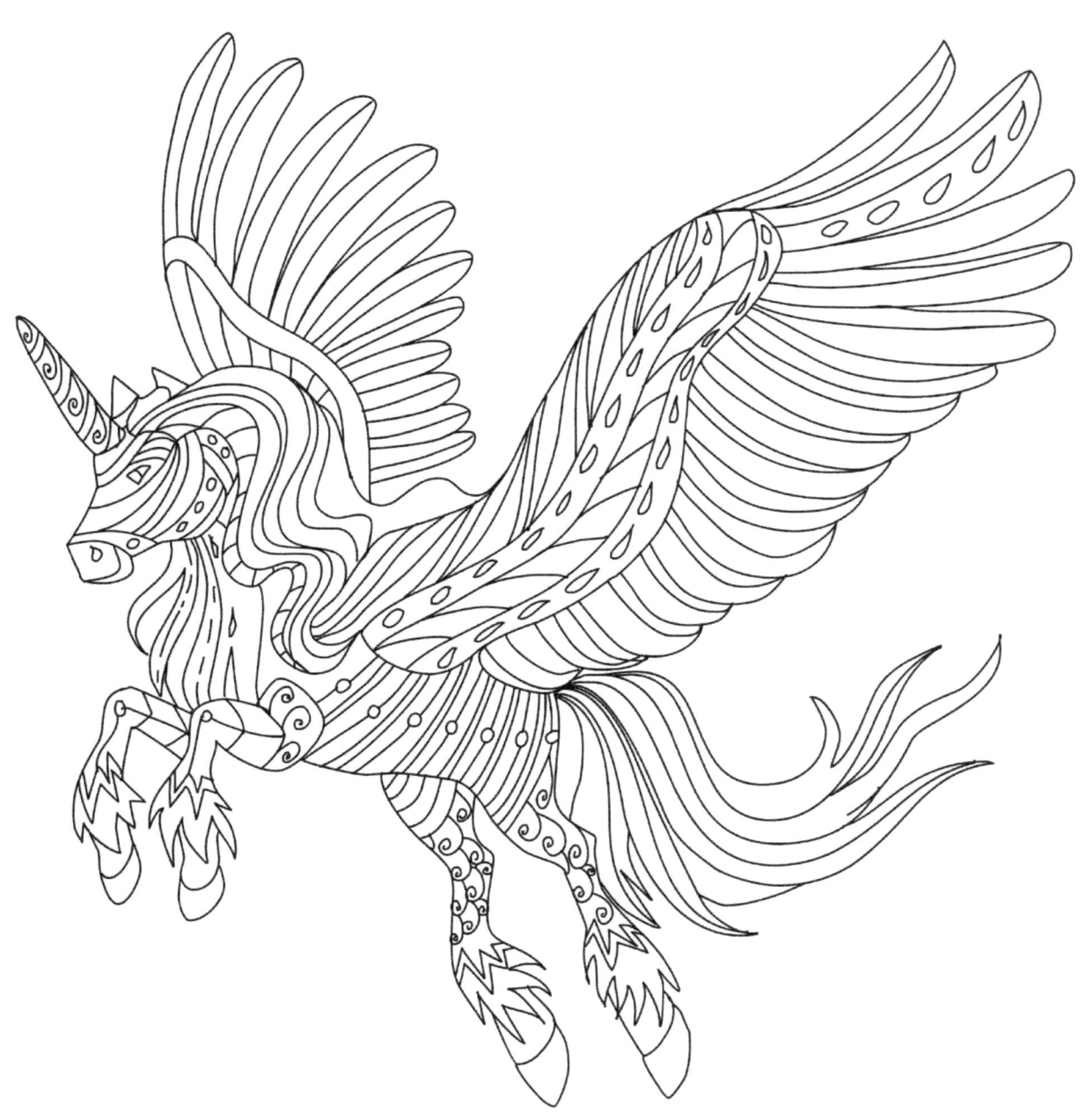

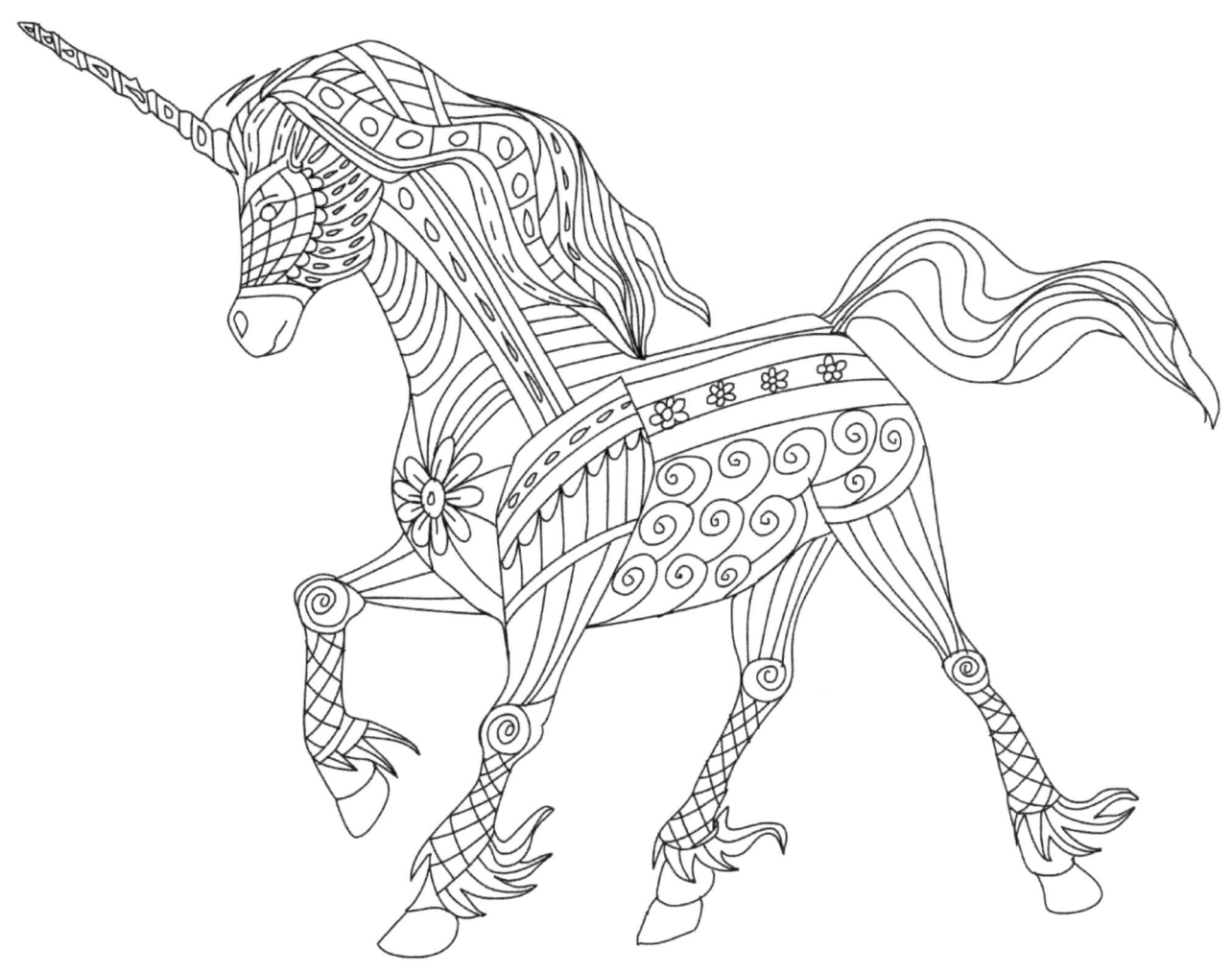

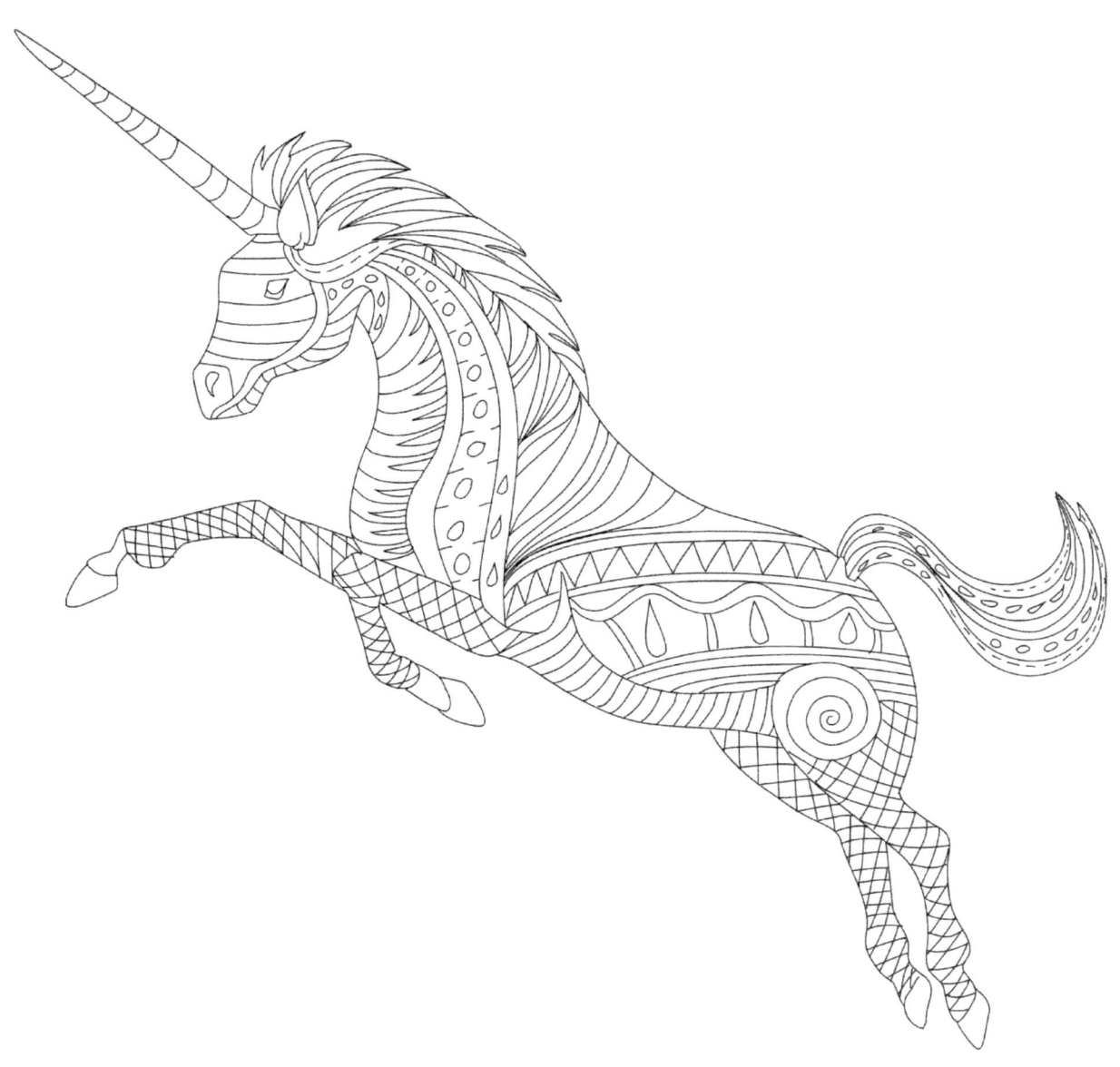

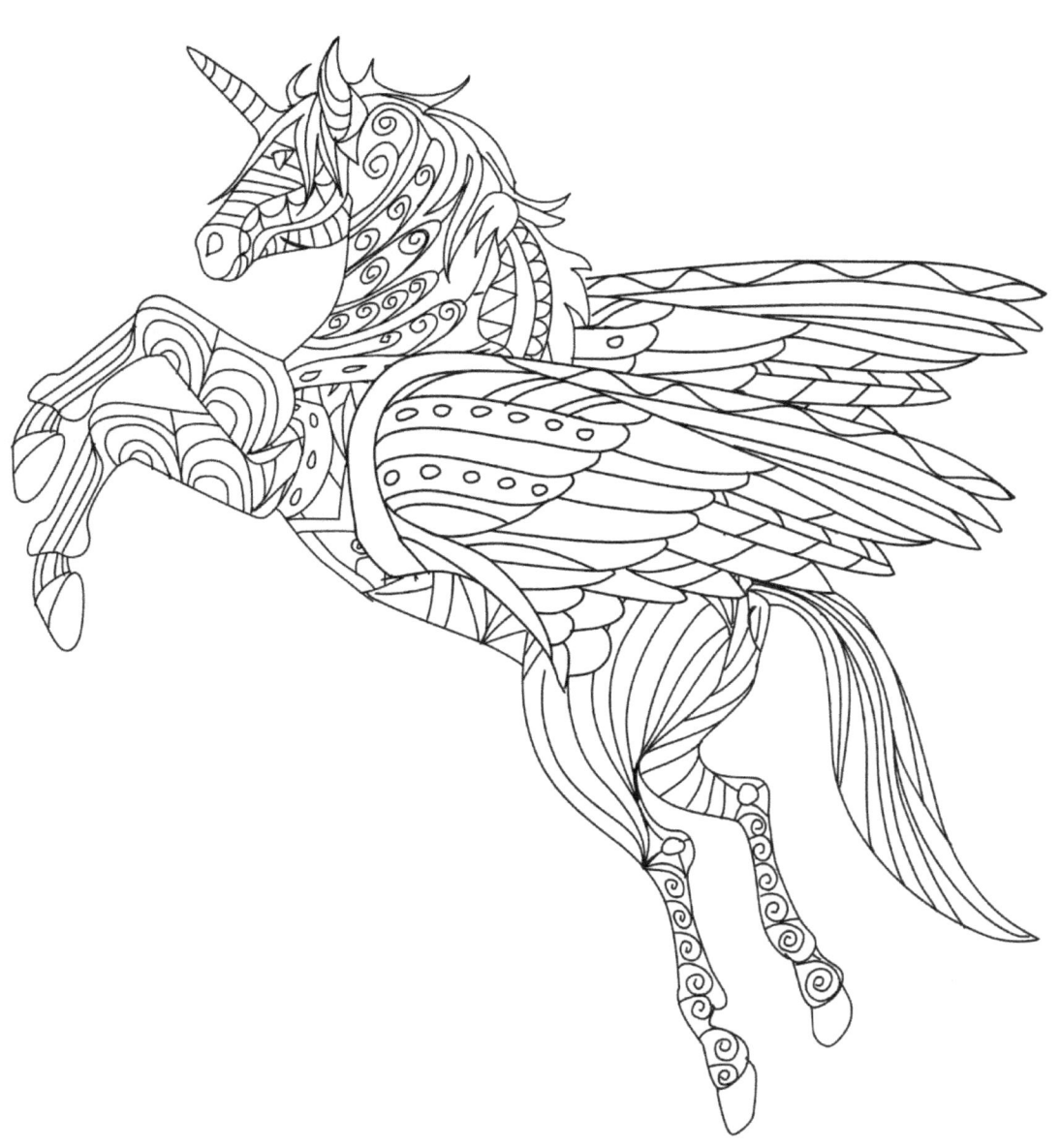

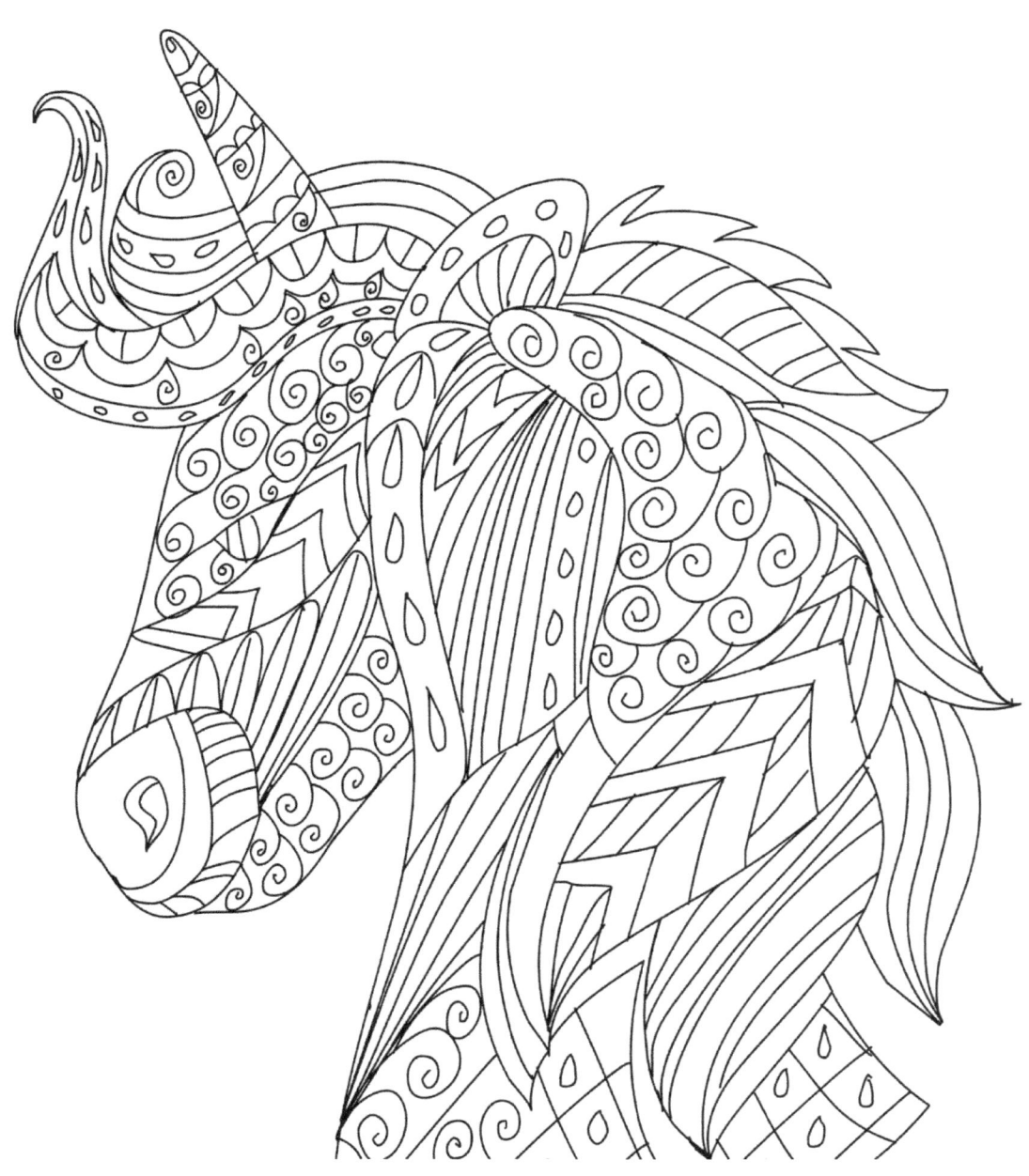

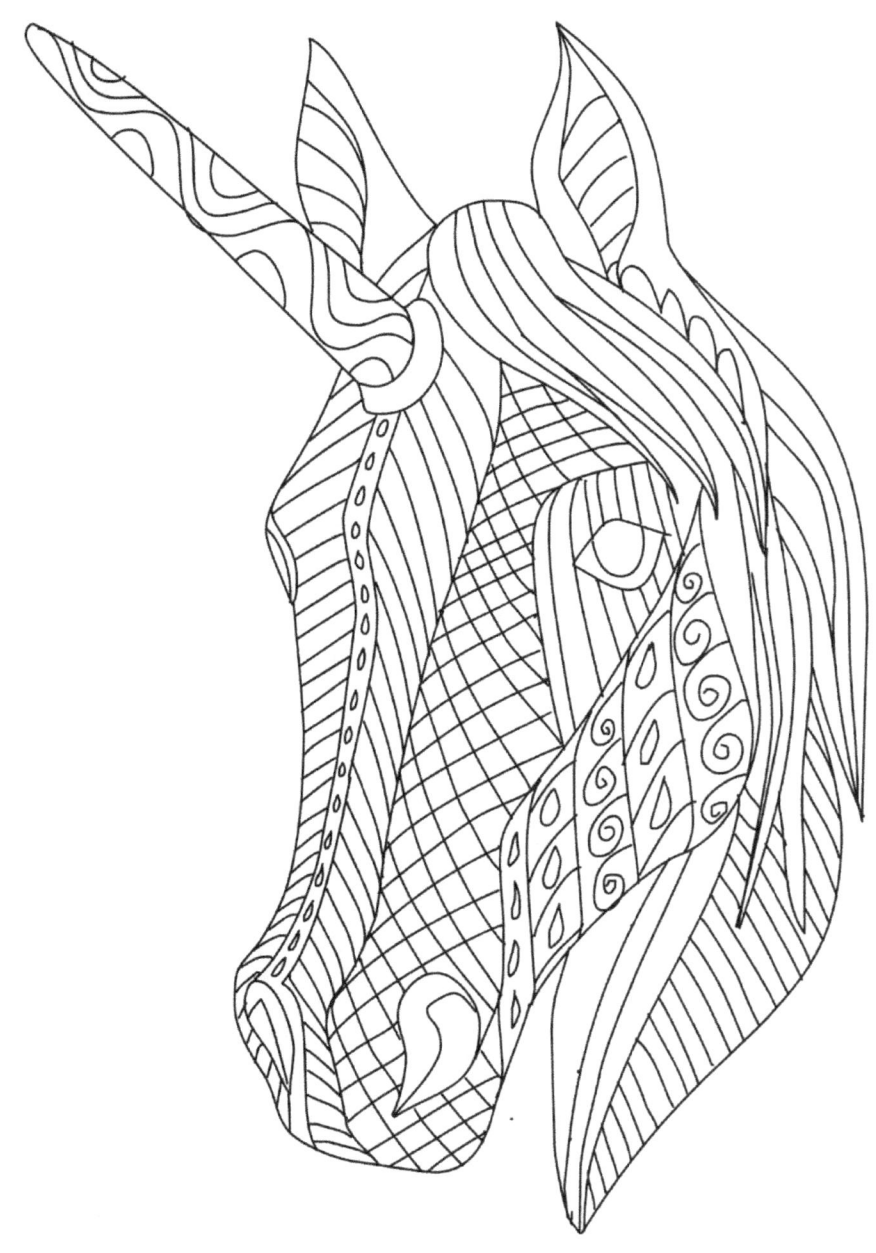

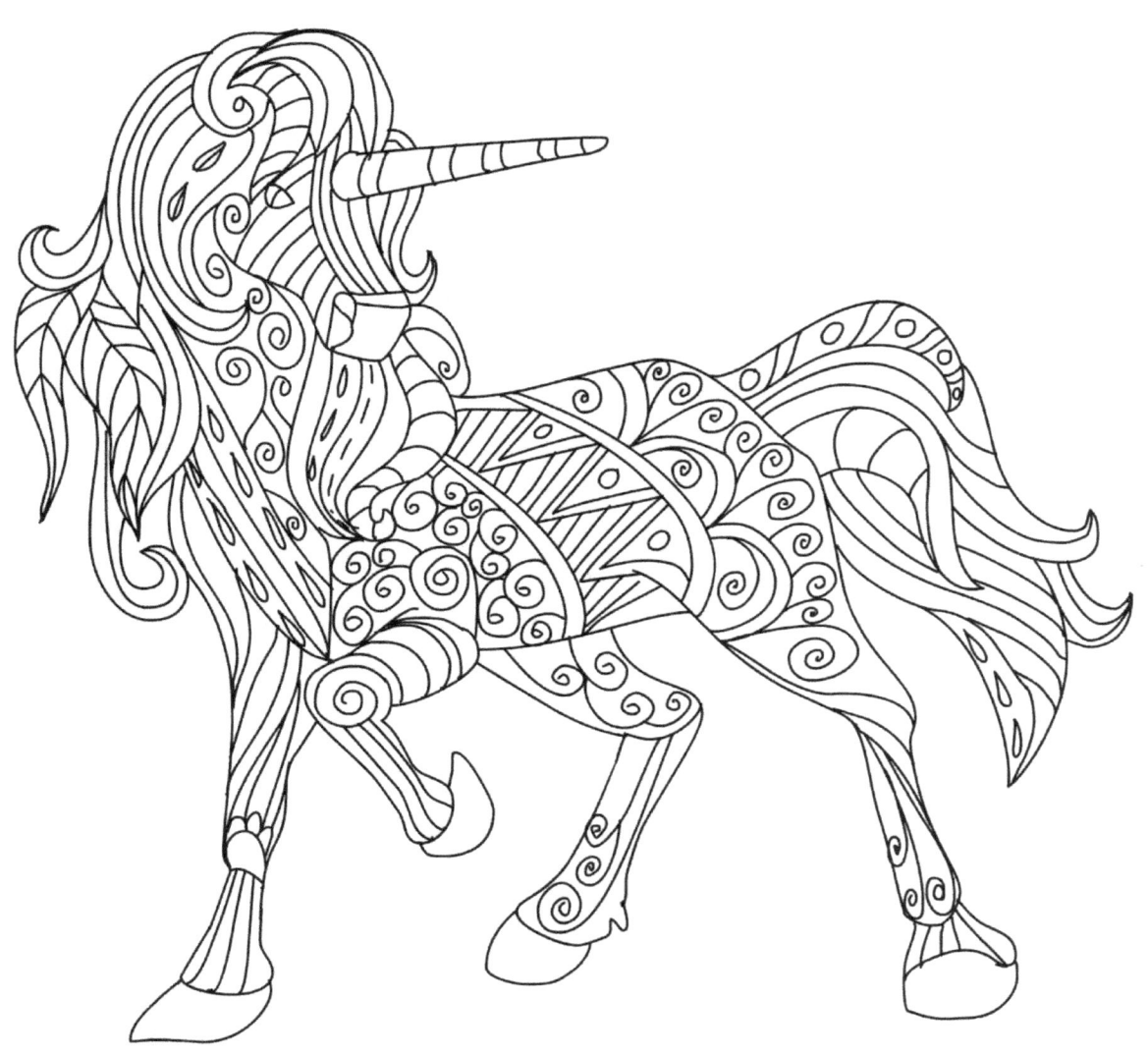

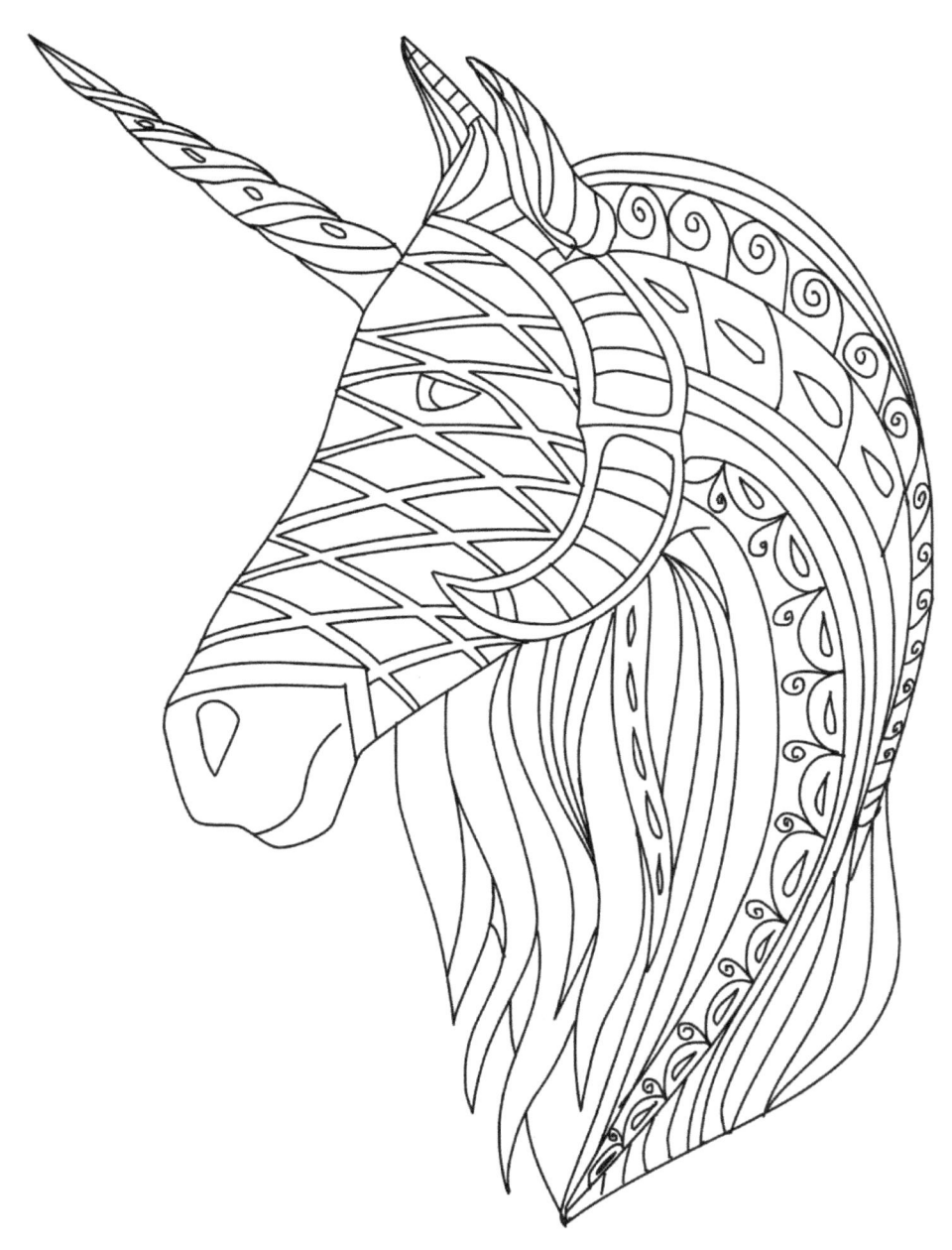